THE MODERN LIBRARY

OF THE WORLD'S BEST BOOKS

THE SELECTED VERSE
OF
OGDEN NASH

*The publishers will be pleased to send, upon request, an
illustrated folder setting forth the purpose and scope of
THE MODERN LIBRARY, and listing each volume
in the series. Every reader of books will find titles he
has been looking for, handsomely printed, in definitive
editions, and at an unusually low price.*

THE SELECTED

VERSE

OF

OGDEN NASH

THE MODERN LIBRARY · NEW YORK

Random House IS THE PUBLISHER OF

THE MODERN LIBRARY

BENNETT A. CERF · DONALD S. KLOPFER · ROBERT K. HAAS

Manufactured in the United States of America
By H. Wolff

CONTENTS

Allow Me, Madam, but It Won't Help

ADORABLE is an adjective and womankind is a noun,
   And I often wonder why, although adorable
   womankind elects to talk standing up, it elects to
   put on its coat sitting down.
What is the outstanding characteristic of matinées, tea
   rooms and table d'hôtes?
Women, sitting firmly and uncomfortably on their coats;
Women, at whose talents a contortionist would hesitate
   to scoff,
Because they also sat down on their coats to take them
   off.
What is *savoir-faire*?
It is the ability to pick up eighty-five cents in nickels and
   a lipstick with the right hand while the left hand is
   groping wildly over the back of a chair.
Yes, and if you desire *savoir-faire* that you could balance
   a cup on,
Consider the calmness of a woman trying to get her
   arm into the sleeve of a coat that she has sat down
   on too far up on.
Women are indeed the salt of the earth,
But I fail to see why they daily submit themselves vol-
   untarily to an operation that a man only undergoes
   when he is trying to put on his trousers in an upper
   berth.

Ha! Original Sin!

VANITY, vanity, all is vanity
    That's any fun at all for humanity.
Food is vanity, so is drink,
And undergarments of gossamer pink,
S. J. Perelman, long vacations,
Going abroad, and rich relations,
The kind of engagements you want to keep,
A hundred honors, and twelve hours' sleep.
Vanities all—Oh Worra, worra!
Rooted in Sodom and Gomorrah.

Vanity, vanity, all is vanity
That's any fun at all for humanity.
That is the gist of the prophet's case,
From Bishop Cannon to Canon Chase.
The prophets chant and the prophets chatter,
But somehow it never seems to matter,
For the world hangs on to its ancient sanity
And orders another round of vanity.
Then Hey! for Gomorrah! and Nonny! for Sodom!
Marie! the Chanel model for Modom!

The Terrible People

PEOPLE who have what they want are very fond of telling people who haven't what they want that they really don't want it,

And I wish I could afford to gather all such people into a gloomy castle on the Danube and hire half a dozen capable Draculas to haunt it.

I don't mind their having a lot of money, and I don't care how they employ it,

But I do think that they damn well ought to admit they enjoy it.

But no, they insist on being stealthy

About the pleasures of being wealthy,

And the possession of a handsome annuity

Makes them think that to say how hard it is to make both ends meet is their bounden duity.

You cannot conceive of an occasion

Which will find them without some suitable evasion.

Yes indeed, with arguments they are very fecund;

Their first point is that money isn't everything, and that they have no money anyhow is their second.

Some people's money is merited,

And other people's is inherited,

But wherever it comes from,

They talk about it as if it were something you got pink gums from.

This may well be,

But if so, why do they not relieve themselves of the burden by transferring it to the deserving poor or to me?

Perhaps indeed the possession of wealth is constantly distressing,

But I should be quite willing to assume every curse of wealth if I could at the same time assume every blessing.

The only incurable troubles of the rich are the troubles that money can't cure,

Which is a kind of trouble that is even more troublesome if you are poor.

Certainly there are lots of things in life that money won't buy, but it's very funny—

Have you ever tried to buy them without money?

Song for a Temperature of a Hundred and One

OF ALL God's creatures give me man
    For impractical uniqueness,
He's hardly tenth when it comes to strength,
But he leads the field in weakness.
Distemper suits the ailing dog,
The chicken's content with pip,
But the human race, which sets the pace,
Takes nothing less than grippe.

THEN, hey for the grippe, for the goodly la grippe!
In dogs it's distemper, in chickens it's pip;
But the lords of creation insist at the least
On the germ that distinguishes man from the beast.

The mule with mange is satisfied,
Or hookworm in the South;
And the best-bred kine will stand in line
To get their hoof-and-mouth;
Bubonic cheers the humble rat
As he happily leaves the ship;
When the horse gets botts he thinks it's lots,
But people hold out for grippe.

THEN, hey for the grippe, for the goodly la grippe,
For the frog in the throat and the chap on the lip;
For the ice on the feet and the fire on the brow,
And the bronchial tubes that moo like a cow.
And hey for the ache in the back of the legs,
And the diet of consommé, water and eggs,
For the mustard that sits on your chest like a cactus,
For the doctor you're kindly providing with practus;
And hey for the pants of which you're so fond,
And the first happy day they're allowed to be donned;
For the first day at work, all bundled in wraps,
And last but not least, for the splendid relapse.
So let man meet his Maker, a smile on his lip,
Singing hey, double hey, for the goodly la grippe

Pediatric Reflection

MANY an infant that screams like a calliope
    Could be soothed by a little attention to its
diope.

Portrait of the Artist as a
Prematurely Old Man

IT IS common knowledge to every schoolboy and even
    every Bachelor of Arts,
That all sin is divided into two parts.
One kind of sin is called a sin of commission, and that is
    very important,
And it is what you are doing when you are doing some-
    thing you ortant,
And the other kind of sin is just the opposite and is
    called a sin of omission and is equally bad in the
    eyes of all right-thinking people, from Billy Sunday
    to Buddha,
And it consists of not having done something you shud-
    dha.
I might as well give you my opinion of these two kinds
    of sin as long as, in a way, against each other we
    are pitting them,
And that is, don't bother your head about sins of com-
    mission because however sinful, they must at least
    be fun or else you wouldn't be committing them.

It is the sin of omission, the second kind of sin,
That lays eggs under your skin.
The way you get really painfully bitten
Is by the insurance you haven't taken out and the checks
you haven't added up the stubs of and the appoint-
ments you haven't kept and the bills you haven't
paid and the letters you haven't written.
Also, about sins of omission there is one particularly
painful lack of beauty,
Namely, it isn't as though it had been a riotous red letter
day or night every time you neglected to do your
duty;
You didn't get a wicked forbidden thrill
Every time you let a policy lapse or forgot to pay a bill;
You didn't slap the lads in the tavern on the back and
loudly cry Whee,
Let's all fail to write just one more letter before we go
home, and this round of unwritten letters is on me.
No, you never get any fun
Out of the things you haven't done,
But they are the things that I do not like to be amid,
Because the suitable things you didn't do give you a lot
more trouble than the unsuitable things you did.
The moral is that it is probably better not to sin at all,
but if some kind of sin you must be pursuing,
Well, remember to do it by doing rather than by not
doing.

The Seven Spiritual Ages of
Mrs. Marmaduke Moore

Mrs. Marmaduke Moore, at the age of ten
   (Her name was Jemima Jevons then),
Was the quaintest of little country maids.
Her pigtails slapped on her shoulder blades;
She fed the chickens, and told the truth
And could spit like a boy through a broken tooth.
She could climb a tree to the topmost perch,
And she used to pray in the Methodist church.

At the age of twenty her heart was pure,
And she caught the fancy of Mr. Moore.
He broke his troth (to a girl named Alice),
And carried her off to his city palace,
Where she soon forgot her childhood piety
And joined in the orgies of high society.
Her voice grew English, or, say, Australian,
And she studied to be an Episcopalian.

At thirty our lives are still before us,
But Mr. Moore had a friend in the chorus.
Connubial bliss was overthrown
And Mrs. Moore now slumbered alone.
Hers was a nature that craved affection;
She gave herself up to introspection;
Then, finding theosophy rather dry,
Found peace in the sweet Bahai and Bahai.

Forty! and still an abandoned wife.
She felt old urges stirring to life.
She dipped her locks in a bowl of henna
And booked a passage through to Vienna.
She paid a professor a huge emolument
To demonstrate what his ponderous volume meant.
Returning, she preached to the unemployed
The gospel according to St. Freud.

Fifty! she haunted museums and galleries,
And pleased young men by augmenting their salaries
Oh, it shouldn't occur, but it does occur,
That poets are made by fools like her.
Her salon was full of frangipani,
Roumanian, Russian and Hindustani,
And she conquered par as well as bogey
By reading a book and going Yogi.

Sixty! and time was on her hands—
Maybe remorse and maybe glands.
She felt a need for a free confession,
To publish each youthful indiscretion,
And before she was gathered to her mothers,
To compare her sinlets with those of others,
Mrs. Moore gave a joyous whoop,
And immersed herself in the Oxford group.

That is the story of Mrs. Moore,
As far as it goes. But of this I'm sure—

When seventy stares her in the face
She'll have found some other state of grace.
Mohammed may be her Lord and master,
Or Zeus, or Mithros or Zoroaster.
For when a lady is badly sexed
God knows what god is coming next.

Lines Indited with All the
Depravity of Poverty

ONE way to be very happy is to be very rich
For then you can buy orchids by the quire and
bacon by the flitch.
And yet at the same time
People don't mind if you only tip them a dime.
Because it's very funny
But somehow if you're rich enough you can get away
with spending water like money
While if you're not rich you can spend in one evening
your salary for the year
And everybody will just stand around and jeer.
If you are rich you don't have to think twice about buy-
ing a judge or a horse,
Or a lower instead of an upper, or a new suit, or a
divorce,
And you never have to say When,

And you can sleep every morning until nine or ten,
All of which
Explains why I should like very, very much to be very,
    very rich.

Reflection on a Wicked World

Purity
    Is obscurity.

The Party

Come Arabella, fetch the cake,
    On a dish with silver handles.
Oh mercy! Feel the table shake!
Lucinda, light the candles.

For Mr. Migg is thir-ty,
Is thir---ty,
Is thir-----ty.
The years are crawling over him
Like wee red ants.
Oh, three times ten is thir-ty,
Is for---ty,
Is fif-----ty.
The further off from England
The nearer is to France.

The little flames they bob and jig,
The dining hall is breezy.
Quick! puff your candles, Mr. Migg,
The little flames die easy.
For Mr. Migg is for-ty,
Is for---ty,
Is for-----ty.
The years are crawling over him
Like wee red ants.
Oh four times ten is for-ty,
Is fif---ty,
Is six-----ty,
And creeping through the icing,
The other years advance.

Why, Arabella, here's a ring!
Lucinda, here's a thimble!
For Mr. Migg there's not a thing—
'Tis not, I trust, a symbol!

For Mr. Migg is fif-ty,
Is fif---ty,
Is fif-----ty.
The years are crawling over him
Like wee red ants.
Oh, five times ten is fif-ty,
Is six---ty,
Is seven-----ty.
Lucinda, put the cake away.
We're going to the dance.

More About People

When people aren't asking questions
    They're making suggestions
And when they're not doing one of those
They're either looking over your shoulder or stepping on
    your toes
And then as if that weren't enough to annoy you
They employ you.
Anybody at leisure
Incurs everybody's displeasure.
It seems to be very irking
To people at work to see other people not working,
So they tell you that work is wonderful medicine,
Just look at Firestone and Ford and Edison,
And they lecture you till they're out of breath or some-
    thing
And then if you don't succumb they starve you to death
    or something.
All of which results in a nasty quirk:
That if you don't want to work you have to work to earn
    enough money so that you won't have to work.

Family Court

ONE would be in less danger
        From the wiles of the stranger
If one's own kin and kith
Were more fun to be with.

Seaside Serenade

IT BEGINS when you smell a funny smell,
    And it isn't vanilla or caramel,
And it isn't forget-me-nots or lilies,
Or new-mown hay, or daffy-down-dillies,
And it's not what the barber rubs on father,
And it's awful, and yet you like it rather.
No, it's not what the barber rubs on Daddy,
It's more like an elderly finnan haddie,
Or, shall we say, an electric fan
Blowing over a sardine can.
It smells of seaweed, it smells of clams,
It's as fishy as first-night telegrams,
It's as fishy as millions of fishy fishes,
In spite of which you find it delishes,
You could do with a second helping, please,
And that, my dears, is the ocean breeze.
And pretty soon you observe a pack
Of people reclining upon their back,

And another sight that is very common
Is people reclining upon their abdomen.
And now you lose the smell of the ocean
In the sweetish vapor of sunburn lotion,
And the sun itself seems paler and colder,
Compared to vermilion face and shoulder.
Athletic young men uncover their torso
In the virile way that maidens adore so,
While paunchy uncles, before they bathe them,
In voluminous beach robes modestly swathe them.
The beach is peppered with ladies who look
Like pictures out of a medical book,
Like burlicue queens, like bubble dancers;
Their clothes are riddles complete with answers.
Last, not least, consider the kiddies,
Chirping like crickets and katydiddies,
Splashing, squealing, slithering, crawling,
Cheerful, tearful, boisterous, bawling,
Kiddies in clamorous crowds that swarm
Heavily over your prostrate form,
Callous kiddies who gallop in myriads
'Twixt ardent Apollos and eager Nereids,
Kiddies who bring, as a priceless cup,
Something dead that a wave washed up.
Well, it's each to his taste, and a taste to each;
Shall we saunter down to the bathing beach?

The Strange Case of Mr. Ormantude's Bride

ONCE there was a bridegroom named Mr. Ormantude
    whose intentions were hard to disparage,
Because he intended to make his a happy marriage,
And he succeeded for going on fifty years,
During which he was in marital bliss up to his ears.
His wife's days and nights were enjoyable
Because he catered to every foible;
He went around humming hymns
And anticipating her whims.
Many a fine bit of repartee died on his lips
Lest it throw her anecdotes into eclipse;
He was always silent when his cause was meritorious,
And he never engaged in argument unless sure he was so
    obviously wrong that she couldn't help emerging
    victorious,
And always when in her vicinity
He was careful to make allowances for her femininity;
Were she snappish, he was sweetish,
And of understanding her he made a fetish.
Everybody said his chances of celebrating his golden
    wedding looked good,
But on his golden wedding eve he was competently poi-
    soned by his wife who could no longer stand being
    perpetually understood.

Lines to Be Mumbled at Ovington's

MR. AND Mrs. F. X. Pleasants
      Request the honor of my presence,
On Saturday the twenty-fourth
To watch their daughter, Barbara North,
Succumb in holy matrimony
To Mr. Maximilian Coney.
A murrain on you, Mr. and Mrs. Pleasants!
I hope you turn into friends of Annie Besant's!

Bishop Apse will do the trick;
He's just the kind that mothers pick.
He has a noble velvet voice
That makes a mother's heart rejoice
And fills a mother's handkerchief
With briny evidence of grief.
A murrain on you too, old Bishop Apse!
I hope you get caught in some vicious moral lapse!

The ushers in their coats of black
Will lead old ladies forth and back,
While bridesmaids in their flowery frocks
Bloom round the bride like hollyhocks.
Who knows but what some sidelong glance
Will propagate a new romance?
A murrain on every bridesmaid and every usher!
I hope they all get spattered with oil from a gusher!

I'll wish some wishes for Mr. Coney
In honor of his matrimony.
I wish him moths, I wish him mice,
I wish him cocktails lacking ice.
I wish him a life abrupt and lonely,
I wish him a wife in title only.
A murrain, a murrain upon you, Maximilian!
If I wish you one death before evening I wish you a
billion!

What have I left for Barbara North
Who changes her name on the twenty-fourth?
A hundred theater-ticket stubs,
Matches and corks from supper clubs,
A dozen notes whose theme is If,
Some lipstick on a handkerchief—
A lesser soul of spite would be a harborer;
Not I. No murrain at all upon you, Barbara!

Ms. Found in a Quagmire

UP, UP, lad, time's a-wastin', press the ignition.
If relief is not forthcoming, consult your physician.
Winnow your symptoms, but never discard the chaff,
And consult your physician, your physician deserves a
laugh.
Explain that when you swallow so much as a coddled
egg it sticks like a fishbone

Somewhere behind your wishbone;
Inquire why your eyes of a sudden refuse to be focused,
And what is the sound in your ears like a courting locust.
Your physician's a man of talents;
Ask him whatever became of your sense of balance.
Don't be irked by his suavity;
Tell how you walk with your legs braced wide lest you
    trip over gravity;
Tell him, too, that your gaze is fixed on your shoes as
    you walk, and better to tell him why:
That a too long upward glance would send you headlong
    into the sky.
Tell him straight that on such and such a day
They took the difference between down and up away.
Give him your problem to solve,
Ask him what to hold onto when under your feet you
    can feel the earth revolve;
Every molehill a mountain, every wormhole a crater,
And every step like the step at the top of the escalator
And don't forget
To reveal your discovery that hair can sweat.
Go ahead, tell him;
Release the cat from the bag, let the doctor bell him.
Give the doctor the chart, show him the map and the
    graph;
If relief is not forthcoming, it says right here on the
    label, consult your physician, your physician de-
    serves a laugh.

Invocation

("*Smoot Plans Tariff Ban on
Improper Books*"—News Item)

SENATOR SMOOT (Republican, Ut.)
   Is planning a ban on smut.
Oh root-ti-toot for Smoot of Ut.
And his reverent occiput.
Smite, Smoot, smite for Ut.,
Grit your molars and do your dut.,
Gird up your l--ns,
Smite h-p and th-gh,
We'll all be Kansas
By and by.

Smite, Smoot, for the Watch and Ward,
For Hiram Johnson and Henry Ford,
For Bishop Cannon and John D., Junior,
For Governor Pinchot of Pennsylvunia,
For John S. Sumner and Elder Hays
And possibly Edward L. Bernays,
For Orville Poland and Ella Boole,
For Mother Machree and the Shelton pool.
When smut's to be smitten
Smoot will smite
For G-d, for country,
And Fahrenheit.

Senator Smoot is an institute
Not to be bribed with pelf;
He guards our homes from erotic tomes
By reading them all himself.
Smite, Smoot, smite for Ut.,
They're smuggling smut from Balt. to Butte!
Strongest and sternest
Of your s-x
Scatter the scoundrels
From Can. to Mex.!

Smite, Smoot, for Smedley Butler,
For any good man by the name of Cutler,
Smite for the W.C.T.U.,
For Rockne's team and for Leader's crew,
For Florence Coolidge and Admiral Byrd,
For Billy Sunday and John D., Third,
For Grantland Rice and for Albie Booth,
For the Woman's Auxiliary of Duluth,
Smite, Smoot,
Be rugged and rough,
Smut if smitten
Is front-page stuff.

Reflection on Babies

A BIT of talcum
Is always walcum.

A Beginner's Guide to the Ocean

LET us now consider the ocean.
It is always in motion.
It is generally understood to be the source of much of
our rain,
And ten thousand fleets are said to have swept over it in
vain.
When the poet requested it to break break break on its
cold gray rocks it obligingly broke broke broke.
Which as the poet was Alfred Lord Tennyson didn't sur-
prise him at all but if it had been me I would prob-
ably have had a stroke.
Some people call it the Atlantic and some the Pacific or
the Antarctic or the Indian or the Mediterranean
Sea,
But I always say what difference does it make, some old
geographer mumbling a few words over it, it will
always be just the Ocean to me.
There is an immortal dignity about something like the
Atlantic,

Which seems to drive unimmortal undignified human
    beings frustratedly frantic.
Just give them one foot on the beach and people who
    were perfectly normal formerly, or whilom,
Why, they are subject to whoops and capers that would
    get them blackballed from an asylum;
Yet be they never so rampant and hollerant,
The ocean is tolerant,
Except a couple of times a day it gives up in disgust and
    goes off by itself and hides,
And that, my dears, accounts for the tides.

A Lady Thinks She Is Thirty

UNWILLINGLY Miranda wakes,
    Feels the sun with terror,
One unwilling step she takes,
    Shuddering to the mirror.

Miranda in Miranda's sight
    Is old and gray and dirty;
Twenty-nine she was last night;
    This morning she is thirty.

Shining like the morning star,
    Like the twilight shining,

Haunted by a calendar,
Miranda sits a-pining.

Silly girl, silver girl,
Draw the mirror toward you;
Time who makes the years to whirl
Adorned as he adored you.

Time is timelessness for you;
Calendars for the human;
What's a year, or thirty, to
Loveliness made woman?

Oh, Night will not see thirty again,
Yet soft her wing, Miranda;
Pick up your glass and tell me, then—
How old is Spring, Miranda?

Introspective Reflection

I WOULD live all my life in nonchalance and insouci-
ance
Were it not for making a living, which is rather a
nouciance.

Do, Do, Do What You Done, Done, Done Before, Before, Before

THERE is a man whose name must be, I think, Mr. Oglethrip, and if you will bring me his head on a silver charger I will award you the hand of my daughter and a lien on my future salary,

And nobody has ever seen him but when you go to an amateur performance of any kind he is always sitting in the upper left-hand corner of the gallery,

And he has the hands of a blacksmith and a heart full of enthusiasm,

And compared to the rest of the audience, well Mr. Oglethrip is not as chusiasm,

Because seasoned amateur performance attenders generally weigh their applause carefully so as not to be either a spendthrift or a hoarder,

Because unless the performers of any performance are your grandmother or your favorite cousin or something your aim is to applaud just enough to not hurt their feelings and not enough to induce them to duplicate the order,

And some girl who once handed you a cup of cocoa at a church supper appears and renders an imitation of Fanny Brice imitating Gertrude Lawrence,

And your applause preserves the delicate balance between ecstasy and abhorrence,

And she is just about to resign the stage to the next

performer and everything is as right as a couple of trivets,

When hark! What is that thunder in the upper left-hand corner of the gallery, can Mr. Olgethrip be driving rivets?

No, but he is clapping his horny hands and before you can say "Gadzooks,"

Why, the cocoa girl is back with an imitation of Gertrude Lawrence imitating Baby Snooks.

Mr. Oglethrip's cup has no brim,

Mr. Olgethrip is he to whom what is too much for anybody else is never enough for him,

If Mr. Oglethrip heard Will Hays sing "Trees,"

He would want a reprise.

Do you know a picture program that Mr. Oglethrip would find simply peachy?

A double bill in which each picture contained a dual role for Don Ameche.

I think it would be nice

If when you cut off Mr. Oglethrip's head to bring to me on a silver charger you would cut it off twice.

Scram, Lion!

GENTLEMEN, I give you the British Empire,
　　And the late Queen Victoria, by no means a
　　vempire.
Britain and Britons I far from excoriate,
I deeply admire their Poet Laureate,
I prefer an evening with A. P. Herbert
To a sail in the moonlight sipping sherbert,
And I'd rather hear a Savoy opera
Than loll in the tropics cornering copra,
And I think Miss Lillie is quite a card
And I'm all agog over Scotland Yard.
I'm impressed by squires who run for Parliament
And serve their country for a modest emolument.
Yes, I praise their peers and I praise their commoners
Their fogs and faces and other phenomenas;
I'm even sufficiently flibberty-gibberty
To praise their premise of personal liberty.
But bo, I'll hand you the whole shebang
When they start to sling Amurrican slang,
And calculate you will lose your lunch
When you glim an Amurrican joke in *Punch*,
For Piccadilly is less spectacular
Than its torture of transatlantic vernacular.
Then, Bravo, Britain! and Long Live George!
Away with Yorktown and Valley Forge;
I've a spilth of open-mouthed admiration

For a top-hole pukka sahib nation
But nix on our chatter—it can't be did.
Twenty-three, skiddoo!—Yours,

The Candy Kid.

Reflection on the Fallibility of Nemesis

HE who is ridden by a conscience
      Worries about a lot of nonscience;
He without benefit of scruples
His fun and income soon quadruples.

Thoughts Thought on an Avenue

THERE would be far less masculine gaming and booz-
    ing
But for the feminine approach to feminine fashions,
      which is distinctly confusing.
Please correct me if, although I don't think I do, I err;
But it is a fact that a lady wants to be dressed exactly
      like everybody else but she gets pretty upset if she
      sees anybody else dressed exactly like her.
Nothing so infuriates her as a similar hat or dress,

Especially if bought for less,

Which brings up another point which I will attempt to
discuss in my guttural masculine jargon;

Her ideal raiment is costlier than her or her dearest
friend's purse can buy, and at the same time her
own exclusive and amazing bargain.

Psychologists claim that men are the dreamers and
women are the realists,

But to my mind women are the starriest-eyed of ideal-
ists,

Though I am willing to withdraw this charge and gladly
eat it uncomplaineously

If anyone can explain to me how a person can wear a
costume that is different from other people's and
the same as other people's, and more expensive
than other people's and cheaper than other people's,
simultaneously.

For the Most Improbable She

What shall I do with So-and-So?
   She won't say Yes and she won't say No.
She tiptoes around the cunningest traps
With a smile and a murmur of Perhaps.
At nine I'm Darling, at ten I'm You—
Tell me, what is a man to do

When the lady his life is based upon
Likes to be wooed but won't be won?

What shall I do with So-and-So?
She won't say Come and she won't say Go.
I'm on my way, but I don't know where—
I wouldn't care, if I didn't care.
Damn the man who invented the story
That a little suspense is salutory.
I swear, by lipstick and powder puff,
Fun is fun, but enough's enough!

What shall I do with So-and-So?
She confesses that I am her favorite beau;
But let the topic of marriage arise
And see the astonishment in her eyes!
Why am I chosen so to be harried?
Other people have gotten married.
Is every courtship conducted thus
Or is it only confined to us?

What shall I do with So-and-So?
If it isn't Yes it must be No,
But who so apathetic as me
To all the other fish in the sea?
On the other hand there's the other guess—
If it isn't No it must be Yes.
But just to be safe, love, I implore you
To let me give me your answer for you.

The Rabbits

Here's a verse about rabbits
　　That doesn't mention their habits.

Thoughts Thought While Waiting for a Pronouncement from a Doctor, an Editor, a Big Executive, the Department of Internal Revenue or Any Other Momentous Pronouncer

Is Time on my hands? Yes it is, it is on my hands and
　　my face and my torso and my tendons of Achilles,
And frankly, it gives me the willies.
The quarter-hour grows to the half-hour as chime clings
　　to the tail of the preceding chime,
And I am tarred and feathered with Time.
No matter how frantically I shake my hands the hours
　　will not drop off or evaporate,
Nor will even the once insignificant minutes co-operate.
The clock has stopped at Now, there is no Past, no
　　Future, and oddly enough also no Now,
Only the hot, moist, beaded seconds on the brow,
Only the days and nights in a gluey lump,
And the smothering weeks that stick like a swarm of
　　bees to a stump.
Time stands still, or it moves forward or backward, or at

least it exists, for Ex-Senator Rush Holt, for Doctor
Dafoe, for Simon and Schuster, yes, and for
Schiaparelli,
But for me it is limbo akimbo, an inverted void, a mouse
with its tail pulled out of its mouth through its
belly.
O the world's most honored watch, I haven't been there,
I've been here;
For how long, for one small seventeen-jeweled tick, or
have I been sitting a year?
I'm a speck in infinite space,
Entombed behind my face.
Shall I suddenly start to gyrate, to rotate, to spiral, to
expand through nebular process to a new universe
maybe, or maybe only a galaxy?
But such a Goldbergian scheme to extinguish one lonely
identity seems, well, undersimplified and, if I may
say so, smart-alexy.
Oh, I shall arise and go now, preferably in a purple-and-
gold palanquin,
Borne on the copper shoulders of a Seminole, an Apache,
a Crow and an Algonquin,
And whatever be my heart's desire, be it a new understanding of Time or a cup of dew gathered from
the spring's first jonquil,
Why if none of the other three will bring it to me, why
perhaps the Algonquil.

The Passionate Pagan and the
Dispassionate Public

A Tragedy of the Machine Age

Boys and girls,
  Come out to play,
The moon is shining
Bright as day.

If the moon is shining
Bright as day,
We think that we'll
Stay in and play.

Hey nonny nonny!
Come, Jennie! Come, Johnnie!
The year's adolescent!
The air's effervescent!
It bubbles like Schweppes!
Aren't you going to take steppes?

It's one of the commoner
Vernal phenomena.
You may go wild
Over air that is mild,
But Johnnie and Jennie
Are not having any.

It is Spring! It is Spring!
Let us leap! Let us sing!
Let us claim we have hives
And abandon our wives!
Let us hire violins
To belittle our sins!
Let us loll in a grotto!
Let this be our motto:
Not sackcloth, but satin!
Not Nordic, but Latin!

An epicene voice
Is our amorous choice!
Tell us that Luna
Compares with that cruna.
Away with your capers!
Go peddle your papers!

It is Spring! It is Spring!
On the lea, on the ling!
The frost is dispersed!
Like the buds let us burst!
Let the sap in our veins
Rush like limited trains!
Let our primitive urges
Disgruntle our clergies,
While Bacchus and Pan
Cavort in the van!

Spring is what winter
Always gazinta.
Science finds reasons
For mutable seasons.
Can't you control
That faun in your soul?
Please go and focus
Your whims on a crocus.

It is Spring! Is it Spring?
Let us sing! Shall we sing?
On the lea, on the ling
Shall we sing it is Spring?
Will nobody fling
A garland to Spring?
Oh, hey nonny nonny!
Oh, Jennie! Oh, Johnnie!
Doesn't dove rhyme with love
While the moon shines above?
Isn't May for the wooer
And June for *l'amour?*
No, it couldn't be Spring!
Do not dance! Do not sing!
These birds and these flowers,
These breezes and bowers,
These gay tirra-lirras
Are all done with mirrors!
Hey nonny! Hey nonny!

Hey nonny! Hey nonny!
Hey nonny! Hey nonny!
Hey nonny . . .

My Daddy

I HAVE a funny daddy
    Who goes in and out with me,
And everything that baby does
My daddy's sure to see,
And everything that baby says
My daddy's sure to tell.
You *must* have read my daddy's verse.
I hope he fries in hell.

Suppose He Threw It in Your Face

PLEASE don't anybody ask me to decide anything, I
    do not know a nut from a meg,
Or which came first, the lady or the tiger, or which came
    next, the chicken or the egg.
It takes a man of vision
To make a decision,

And my every memory
Is far too dilemmary.
I am, alas, to be reckoned
With the shortstop who can't decide whether to throw
    to first or second,
Nor can I decide whether to put, except after c,
E before i, or i before e.
But where this twilight mind really goes into eclipse
Is in the matter of tips.
I stand stricken before the triple doom,
Whether, and How Much, and Whom.
Tell me, which is more unpleasant,
The look from him who is superior to a tip and gets it,
    or from him who isn't and doesn't?
I had rather be discovered playing with my toes in the
    Boston Aquarium
Than decide wrongly about an honorarium.
Oh, to dwell forever amid Utopian scenery
Where hotels and restaurants and service stations are
    operated by untippable unoffendable machinery.

A Bas Ben Adhem

MY FELLOW man I do not care for.
    I often ask me, What's he there for?
The only answer I can find
Is, Reproduction of his kind.

If I'm supposed to swallow that,
Winnetka is my habitat.
Isn't it time to carve Hic Jacet
Above that Reproduction racket?

To make the matter more succinct:
Suppose my fellow man extinct.
Why, who would not approve the plan
Save possibly my fellow man?
Yet with a politician's voice
He names himself as Nature's choice.

The finest of the human race
Are bad in figure, worse in face.
Yet just because they have two legs
And come from storks instead of eggs
They count the spacious firmament
As something to be charged and sent.

Though man created smocks and snoods
And one-way streets and breakfast foods,
And double features and mustard plasters,
And Andrews Sisters and Lady Astors,
He hails himself with drum and fife
And bullies lower forms of life.

Not that I think that much depends
On how we treat our feathered friends,

Or claim the wart hog in the zoo
Is nearer God than me or you;
Just that I wonder as I scan
The wherefore of my fellow man.

The Pig

THE pig, if I am not mistaken,
    Supplies us sausage, ham, and bacon.
Let others say his heart is big—
I call it stupid of the pig.

The Individualist

ONCE there was a man named Jarvis Gravel who was
    just a man named Jarvis Gravel except for one
    thing:
He hated spring.
And this was because once a Communist had said Come
    on down to Union Square, it's May Day,
And Jarvis went, thinking he had said Come on down
    to Union Square, it's pay day.
So from then on anything at all vernal
Was to him strictly infernal.

When he saw the first crocus poke its head up
He'd get a shovel and dig the entire bed up,
And he bought a horse and galloped back and forth
Tipping off the worms when the first robin started North.
To love the way of a man with a maid in the moonlight
was something he never learnt,
And he spent a lot of beautiful balmy evenings moving
FRESH PAINT signs from park benches that were
freshly painted to ones that weren't,
And when he finally did marry a girl who made his
pulses quicken
It was merely because her name was Gale Winterbottom
and she was no spring chicken,
And one day during the worm-warning season he came
home hungry after a hard day in the stirrup,
And she served him waffles and he objected to the May-
pole syrup,
So she shot him through the heart, but his last words
were ecstatic.
He said Thank you honey, it was thoughtful of you to
use the autumnatic.

Thunder Over the Nursery

LISTEN to me, angel tot,
Whom I love an awful lot,
It will save a barrel of bother
If we understand each other.

Every time that I'm your herder
You think you get away with murder.
All right, infant, so you do,
But only because I want you to.

Baby's muscles are prodigious,
Baby's beautiful, not higious,
She can talk and walk and run
Like a daughter of a gun.

Well, you may be a genius, child,
And I a parent dull and mild;
In spite of which, and nevertheless,
I could lick you yet, I guess.

Forgive me, pet, if I am frank,
But truth is money in the bank;
I wish you to admire and love yourself,
But not to get too far above yourself.

When we race, you always win;
Baby, think before you grin.

It may occur to you, perhaps,
That Daddy's running under wraps.

When you hide behind the chair
And Daddy seeks you everywhere,
Behind the door, beneath the bed—
That's Daddy's heart, not Baby's head.

When I praise your speech in glee
And claim you talk as well as me,
That's the spirit, not the letter.
I know more words, and say them better.

In future, then, when I'm your herder,
Continue getting away with murder;
But know from him who murder endures,
It's his idea much more than yours.

Reflections on Ice-Breaking

CANDY
Is dandy
But liquor
Is quicker.

Dragons Are Too Seldom

To ACTUALLY see an actual marine monster
Is one of the things that I do before I die I wonster.
Should you ask me if I desire to meet the bashful inhabi-
tant of Loch Ness,
I could only say yes.
Often my eye with moisture dims
When I think that it has never been my good fortune to
gaze on one of Nature's whims.
Far from ever having seen a Gorgon
I haven't even seen the midget that sat in the lap of Mr.
Morgan.
Indeed it is my further ill fortune or mishap
That far from having seen the midget that sat in it I have
never even seen Mr. Morgan's lap.
Indeed I never much thought about Mr. Morgan's hav-
ing a lap because just the way you go into churches
and notice the stained glass more than the apses
When you think about multi-millionaires you don't think
about their laps as much as their lapses;
But it seems that they do have laps which is one human
touch that brings them a little closer to me and you,
And maybe they even go so far as to sometimes have hiccups too.
But regular monsters like sea serpents don't have laps or
hiccups or any other characteristic that is human,
And I would rather see a second-rate monster such as a
mermaid than a first-rate genius such as John Bun-

yan or Schiaparelli or Schubert or Schumann;
Yes, I would rather see one of the sirens
Than two Lord Byrons,
And if I knew that when I got there I could see Cyclops
or Scylla and Charybdis or Pegasus
I would willingly walk on my hands from here to Dallas,
Tegasus,
Because I don't mean to be satirical,
But where there's a monster there's a miracle,
And after a thorough study of current affairs, I have
concluded with regret
That the world can profitably use all the miracles it can
get,
And I think life would be a lot less demoralizing,
If instead of sitting around in front of the radio listening
to torture singers sing torture songs we sat around
listening to the Lorelei loreleising.

Lines to a Three-Name Lady

MRS. HATTIE BOOMER SPINK,
  You puzzle me a lot.
Do you, I wonder, ever think?
And, if you do, of what?

Oh, solons bow like slender reeds
Beneath your firm resolve.

Your words I know, I know your deeds—
But whence do they evolve?

Do you employ a cerebrum,
And eke a cerebellum?
Or do you simply let 'em come,
With Gabriel at the hellum?

Nay, show me not your LL.D.
From Oklahoma Christian;
This honorary verdegree
Doth only beg the question.

Your native mental processes
Imply some secret canker;
Instead of thoughts, antipathies;
Instead of reason, rancor.

The ripple in your skull that spreads
From some primeval pebble,
How quickly washes o'er the heads
Of prophet and of rebel!

You three-name women, Mrs. Spink,
You puzzle me a lot.
Do you, I wonder, ever think?
And if you do, of what?

When gossip first began to link
Your name with that of Mr. Spink,
O Hattie Boomer, did you think?
—And what's become of Mr. Spink?

Funebrial Reflection

AMONG the anthropophagi
People's friends are people's sarcophagi.

I Don't Mean Us, Except Occasionally

I KNOW a man who when he bares his breast to life it
comes back to him all covered with welts,
Because everything that happens to him is much worse
than the same thing happening to anybody else.
Other people with a cold just have colds, but when he
has a cold it combines pneumonia and dropsy and
tropical fever,
And he greets any attempt to cheer him up with the
frigid politeness of a retiring Chairman of the Board
saying How do you do to the newly appointed
Receiver.

Other people with indigestion just have indigestion, but his indigestion ranks somewhere between appendicitis and cholera,

And his medicine chest is clogged with various gastric appeasers costing from fifty cents a bottle up to a dollar a.

He is the man for whom the razor-blade people manufacture that special individual teaspoon-edged blade for,

And the man who never discovers that his new shoes don't fit until immediately after they are paid for.

Everybody is always running around with bushels with which to hide his talents,

And he is the only depositor in the world for whom his bank employs a special staff of certified private accountants just to keep his bank book out of balance.

I really don't see how that man remains perpendicular,

And I am glad that I am not at all like him, except in many a particular.

The Life of the Party

Lily, there isn't a thing you lack,
    Your effect is simply stunning.
But Lily, your gown is low in the back,
So conduct yourself with cunning.
Some of your charm is charm of face,
But some of your charm is spinal;
Losing your looks is no disgrace,
But losing your poise is final.
Ridicule's name is Legion,
So look to your dorsal region.

For Artie,
Old Artie,
The life of the party,
Is practically perfect tonight;
He's prettily, properly tight;
He's never appeared so bright.
Have you ever seen Artie
Enliven a party?
You've never seen Artie—
Why Lord love a duck!
At present old Artie is running amuck.
There's a wink in his eye
And a smile on his lips
For the matron he tickles,
The waiter he trips.

There's a rubber cigar,
And a smoking-room jest,
To melt the reserve
Of the clerical guest.
There's a pin for the man who stoops over,
And a little trained flea for Rover.
So Lily, beware of your back!
More daring than duller and older blades,
Artie is hot on the track.
I've noticed him eying your shoulder blades.
And maybe it's salad,
And maybe it's ice,
But I fear he has planned
Some amusing device,
For the laughter is slack
And he's taking it hard—
He's eying your back—
And Artie's a card—
He's forming a plan—
May I fetch you a shawl?
That inventive young man—
There is one in the hall.
Though your back is divine
In its natural state,
May I curtain your spine?—
Dear Heaven, I'm late!
Aren't you glad that you came to the party?
And weren't you amused by Artie?

Horace, the moment that you appeared,
I admired your manly beauty,
But I feel that a word about your beard
Is only my bounden duty.
Your tailor's craft is a dandy's dream,
Your suavity leaves me lyrical,
But escaping tonight with your self-esteem
Will require a minor miracle.
Fun is a gay deceiver,
So look to your kingly beaver.

For Artie,
Old Artie,
The life of the party,
Is hitting his stride tonight.
No bushel obscures his light.
He's knocking them left and right.
Have you ever seen Artie
Enliven a party?
You've never seen Artie—
My lad, you're in luck,
For Artie, old Artie, is running amuck.
At Artie's approach
Lesser wags droop.
Have you seen the tin roach
He drops in your soup?
Is a spoon in your pocket?
Or gum on your chair?
It's Artie, old Artie,

Who magicked them there.
And of those who complain, there's a rumor
That they're lacking in sense of humor.
So Horace, beware of your beard!
I scent some fantastic flubdubbery!
Old Artie has just disappeared
And I've noticed him eying your shrubbery.
And maybe it's syrup,
And maybe it's mice,
But I fear he has planned
Some amusing device.
His conceptions are weird,
And nothing is barred—
He was eying your beard—
And Artie's a card—
When Artie returns,
The fun will begin—
May I fetch you a bag
To put on your chin?
Just a small paper bag
To envelop the bait?
For Artie's a wag—
Dear Heaven, I'm late!
Aren't you glad that you came to the party?
And weren't you amused by Artie?

The Cow

THE cow is of the bovine ilk;
    One end is moo, the other, milk.

That Reminds Me

JUST imagine yourself seated on a shadowy terrace,
    And beside you is a girl who stirs you more
      strangely than an heiress.
It is a summer evening at its most superb,
And the moonlight reminds you that To Love is an active
      verb,
And your hand clasps hers, which rests there without
      shrinking,
And after a silence fraught with romance you ask her
      what she is thinking,
And she starts and returns from the moon-washed dis-
      tances to the shadowy veranda,
And says, Oh I was wondering how many bamboo shoots
      a day it takes to feed a baby Giant Panda.
Or you stand with her on a hilltop and gaze on a winter
      sunset,
And everything is as starkly beautiful as a page from
      Sigrid Undset,
And your arm goes round her waist and you make an
      avowal which for masterfully marshaled emotional

content might have been a page of Ouida's or
Thackeray's,
And after a silence fraught with romance she says, I forgot to order the limes for the Daiquiris.
Or in a twilight drawing room you have just asked the
most momentous of questions,
And after a silence fraught with romance she says I think
this little table would look better where that little
table is, but then where would that little table go,
have you any suggestions?
And that's the way they go around hitting below our
belts;
It isn't that nothing is sacred to them, it's just that at the
Sacred Moment they are always thinking of something else.

After the Christening

Come along, everybody, see the pretty baby,
Such a pretty baby ought to be adored.
Come along, everybody, come and bore the baby,
See the pretty baby, begging to be bored.

Hurry, hurry, Aunt Louise,
Silly names are sure to please.
Bother what the baby thinks!

Call her Kitchy-kitch and Binks,
Call her Wackywoo and Snookums,
Just ignore her dirty lookums,
Who than she is fairer game
For every kind of silly name?
Baby cannot answer back,
Or perhaps an aunt she'd lack.

Come along, everybody, isn't she a darling?
Such a little darling ought to be enjoyed.
Come along, everybody, let's annoy the baby,
Such a darling darling begs to be annoyed.

Goodness Gracious, Uncle George!
Home at last from Valley Forge?
Won't you try on her the whoops
That cheered the Continental troops?
Stand a little closer, please;
That will put her at her ease;
And babies find it hard to hear,
So place your mouth against her ear—
I guess she heard it, Uncle George;
I'm sure they did at Valley Forge.

Come along, everybody, see the little lady,
Isn't she adorable and kissable and pleasing?
Come along, everybody, come and tease the baby,
Here's a lady baby available for teasing!

Cousin Charles was always chummy;
He's about to poke her tummy.
Grandpa almost chokes on chuckles,
Tickling with his beard her knuckles;
All of Granny's muscles ache
From half an hour of patty-cake;
God-mamma with glee begins
A noisy count of baby's chins;
God-papa with humor glows
Playing piggie with her toes.
See the happy prideful parents,
Do they think of interference?
Certainly not, while baby gives
Such wholesome fun to relatives.
Up and at her, everybody, at the pretty baby,
Tell her she's a dumpling, tell her she's a dear.
Everybody knows the way to woo a baby—
Tickle her and pinch her and yodel in her ear.

The Germ

A MIGHTY creature is the germ,
 Though smaller than the pachyderm.
His customary dwelling place
Is deep within the human race.
His childish pride he often pleases
By giving people strange diseases.
Do you, my poppet, feel infirm?
You probably contain a germ.

I Know You'll Like Them

YOU don't need to study any ponderous tome
 To find out how to make your out-of-town guests
  feel not at home,
Because there is one way which couldn't be exquisiter
For enthralling the visitor.
You plan a little gathering informal and sociable
And you ask a few friends whose manners are irre-
  proaciable,
And you speak up with all the pride of Mr. Dewey an-
  nouncing a couple of important impending arrests,
And you say Friends, this is Mr. and Mrs. Comfitmonger,
  my out-of-town guests,
And you even amplify your introduction so as to break
  the ice with more velocity,

And you tell them that Mrs. Comfitmonger used to be a
　　policewoman and Mr. Comfitmonger is a piano tuner
　　of no mean virtuosity,

And you hint that Mr. Comfitmonger has had some
　　pretty intriguing experiences in his years as a vir-
　　tuoso,

And that Mrs. Comfitmonger while pounding her beat
　　has dealt with personalities who would scare the
　　pants off Lombroso,

And that everything is all set for a dandy evening of gen-
　　eral chitchat is what you think,

And you retire to the pantry to prepare everybody a
　　drink,

And you hear the brouhaha of vivacious voices,

And your heart rejoices,

Because it seems that your friends find Mr. Comfitmon-
　　ger's anecdotes of life under the Steinways fascinat-
　　ing,

And are spellbound by Mrs. Comfitmonger's articulate
　　opposition to arson and assassinating,

And you say This party is indeed de luxe,

And you emerge to find all your friends excitedly dis-
　　cussing putts that wouldn't go down and stocks that
　　wouldn't go up, and Mr. and Mrs. Comfitmonger
　　over in a corner leafing·through your books,

And if you think you can turn the conversation to Pales-
　　trina or police work,

You've taken on a mighty pretty job of piecework,

Because if there is one thing in which everybody's home-
    team friends are unerring,
It is to confine their conversation to mutual acquaint-
    ances and episodes as to which your visiting friends
    have no idea of to what they are referring.
Most people are only vocal
When talking local.

Pretty Halcyon Days

How pleasant to sit on the beach,
    On the beach, on the sand, in the sun,
With ocean galore within reach,
And nothing at all to be done!
No letters to answer,
No bills to be burned,
No work to be shirked,
No cash to be earned.
It is pleasant to sit on the beach
With nothing at all to be done.

How pleasant to look at the ocean,
Democratic and damp; indiscriminate;
It fills me with noble emotion
To think I am able to swim in it.
To lave in the wave,
Majestic and chilly,

Tomorrow I crave;
But today it is silly.
It is pleasant to look at the ocean;
Tomorrow, perhaps, I shall swim in it.

How pleasant to gaze at the sailors,
As their sailboats they manfully sail
With the vigor of vikings and whalers
In the days of the viking and whale.
They sport on the brink
Of the shad and the shark;
If it's windy they sink;
If it isn't, they park.
It is pleasant to gaze at the sailors,
To gaze without having to sail.

How pleasant the salt anæsthetic
Of the air and the sand and the sun;
Leave the earth to the strong and athletic,
And the sea to adventure upon.
But the sun and the sand
No contractor can copy;
We lie in the land
Of the lotus and poppy;
We vegetate, calm and æsthetic,
On the beach, on the sand, in the sun.

Reflections on Ingenuity

Here's a good rule of thumb:
Too clever is dumb.

No Doctors Today, Thank You

They tell me that euphoria is the feeling of feeling
wonderful, well, today I feel euphorian,
Today I have the agility of a Greek god and the appetite
of a Victorian.
Yes, today I may even go forth without my galoshes,
Today I am a swashbuckler, would anybody like me to
buckle any swashes?
This is my euphorian day,
I will ring welkins and before anybody answers I will
run away.
I will tame me a caribou
And bedeck it with marabou.
I will pen me my memoirs.
Ah youth, youth! What euphorian days them was!
I wasn't much of a hand for the boudoirs,
I was generally to be found where the food was.
Does anybody want any flotsam?
I've gotsam.
Does anybody want any jetsam?

I can getsam.
I can play chopsticks on the Wurlitzer,
I can speak Portuguese like a Berlitzer.
I can don or doff my shoes without tying or untying the
    laces because I am wearing moccasins,
And I practically know the difference between serums
    and antitoccasins.
Kind people, don't think me purse-proud, don't set me
    down as vainglorious;
I'm just a little euphorious.

Happy Days, Elmer!

ELMER stops me in the street,
    He fastens to my arm;
Elmer's words are words of heat,
I view him with alarm.
Elmer's eyes are eyes that glisten;
When he talks, he pants;
To Elmer's speech I do not listen;
Know it in advance.

Somewhere, somehow, something terrible,
Something altogether unbearable,
Squashes a premier, squashes a homebody,
Something dreadful happens to somebody.

Bombs are exploding like banks,
Banks are exploding like bombs,
Senators swallow their planks,
Kippurs are torn from their Yoms.
The world is adrift in a fog;
Myself, I am frankly appalled;
But Elmer is gayly agog;
Yes, Elmer is simply enthralled.
Says Elmer, the times are portentous,
We are favored to be on the spot
At a moment, he says, so momentous—
I trust he's momentously shot.

Elmer passes in the street,
I take him by the arm;
Elmer must have grown effete;
He views me with alarm.
Elmer's eyes are eyes that pop;
When I talk, he pants;
I orate without a stop;
Prepared it in advance.

Somewhere, somehow, something tedious,
Something stupidly yes-indeedious,
Something tiresome will happen to somebody,
Bore a celebrity, weary a homebody.
PM will yawn at The News,
The Dodgers lie down with the Giants,
Dictators will huddle in zoos,

And business will boom at Lane Bryant's.
Nothing will rise or fall
In a humdrum world and drowsy.
Elmer won't like it at all,
But life will be much less lousy.
I'm ragged from critical crises,
And I beg with my vanishing breath,
At the moment, O Lord, I want to be bored—
I want to be bored to death!

The Duck

BEHOLD the duck.
It does not cluck.
A cluck it lacks.
It quacks.
It is specially fond
Of a puddle or pond.
When it dines or sups,
It bottoms ups.

Now You See It, Now I Don't

SOME people look to the future and others look days of
   yore-wards,

But even they see more eye to eye than two people on a
   train one of whom is riding backwards and the other
   forwards.

I don't know how it does or when,

But anything interesting described by a forwards rider
   has vanished by the time it should have swum into
   the backwards rider's ken,

While, through a freak twist of the current

The backwards rider gets to see a lot of interesting things
   that should have been there a moment ago for the
   forwards rider to see but somehow they just wur-
   rent.

Travelers have told me and I have believed them,

That such noticeable objects as the Mississippi River and
   the Sierra Nevada mountains have disappeared between the time when the forwards rider pointed
   them out and the backwards rider should have per-
   ceived them.

There are those who in an effort to explain this phe-
   nomenon have developed a disturbing knack;

They sit forwards and look back,

While others to whom their vertebræ are dearer

Sit backwards and gaze on the fleeting landscape through
   a mirror.

But no matter what they describe

Their accounts never jibe.
When I eventually establish my Universal Travel Service
and Guide Ways
I shall advise all my clients who really want to see anything just to sit at home and look sideways.

The Big Tent Under the Roof

Noises new to sea and land
    Issue from the circus band.
Each musician looks like mumps
From blowing umpah umpah umps.

Lovely girls in spangled pants
Ride on gilded elephants.
Elephants are useful friends,
They have handles on both ends;
They hold each other's hindmost handles
And flee from mice and Roman candles.
Their hearts are gold, their hides are emery,
And they have a most tenacious memory.

Notice also, girls and boys,
The circus horses' avoirdupois.
Far and wide the wily scouts
Seek these snow-white stylish stouts.

Calmer steeds were never found
Unattached to a merry-go-round.
Equestriennes prefer to jump
Onto horses pillow-plump.

Equestriennes will never ride
As other people do, astride.
They like to balance on one foot,
And wherever they get, they won't stay put.
They utter frequent whoops and yips,
And have the most amazing hips.
Pink seems to be their favorite color,
And very few things are very much duller.

Yet I for one am more than willing
That everything should be less thrilling.
My heart and lungs both bound and balk
When high-wire walkers start to walk.
They ought to perish, yet they don't;
Some fear they will, some fear they won't.

I lack the adjectives, verbs and nouns
To do full justice to the clowns.
Their hearts are constantly breaking, I hear,
And who am I to interfere?
I'd rather shake hands with Mr. Ringling
And tell him his circus is a beautiful thingling.

The Camel

THE camel has a single hump;
   The dromedary, two;
Or else the other way around.
I'm never sure. Are you?

"Tomorrow, Partly Cloudy"

RAINY vacations
   Try people's patience.
To expect rain in the autumn
Experience has tautumn,
And rain in the spring and winter
Makes no stories for the printer,
But rain on summer colonies
Breeds misdemeanors and felonies.
Summer cottages are meant just to sleep in,
Not to huddle all day in a heap in,
And whether at sea level or in higher places
There are not enough fireplaces,
And the bookcase stares at you starkly
And seems to be full of nothing but Volume II of the life
   of Rutherford B. Hayes, and *The Rosary*, by Flor-
   ence M. Barclay,

And everybody wishes they had brought woolens and
    tweeds instead of linens and foulards,
And if you succeed in lining up four for bridge the only
    deck turns out to have only fifty-one cards,
And tennis rackets grow frazzled and golf sticks rusty
    and bathing suits moldy,
And parents grow scoldy,
And on all sides you hear nothing but raindrops going
    sputter-sput, sputter-sput,
And bureau drawers won't open and bathroom doors
    won't shut,
And all attempts at amusement fail,
Even reading the previous tenants' jettisoned mail,
Although naturally it would never have been jettisoned
If it hadn't been reticent.
But you could stand everything if it wasn't for one ma-
    lignant committee,
Which is the one that turns the sun on again just as you
    are leaving for the city.
Yes indeed, rainy vacations
Certainly try people's patience.

Song to Be Sung by the Father
of Infant Female Children

MY HEART leaps up when I behold
   A rainbow in the sky;
Contrariwise, my blood runs cold
When little boys go by.
For little boys as little boys,
No special hate I carry,
But now and then they grow to men,
And when they do, they marry.
No matter how they tarry,
Eventually they marry.
And, swine among the pearls,
They marry little girls.

Oh, somewhere, somewhere, an infant plays,
With parents who feed and clothe him.
Their lips are sticky with pride and praise,
But I have begun to loathe him.
Yes, I loathe with a loathing shameless
This child who to me is nameless.
This bachelor child in his carriage
Gives never a thought to marriage,
But a person can hardly say knife
Before he will hunt him a wife.

I never see an infant (male),
A-sleeping in the sun,

Without I turn a trifle pale
And think, is *he* the one?
Oh, first he'll want to crop his curls,
And then he'll want a pony,
And then he'll think of pretty girls
And holy matrimony.
He'll put away his pony,
And sigh for matrimony.
A cat without a mouse
Is he without a spouse.

Oh, somewhere he bubbles bubbles of milk,
And quietly sucks his thumbs.
His cheeks are roses painted on silk,
And his teeth are tucked in his gums.
But alas, the teeth will begin to grow,
And the bubbles will cease to bubble;
Given a score of years or so,
The roses will turn to stubble.
He'll sell a bond, or he'll write a book,
And his eyes will get that acquisitive look,
And raging and ravenous for the kill,
He'll boldly ask for the hand of Jill.
This infant whose middle
Is diapered still
Will want to marry
My daughter Jill.

Oh sweet be his slumber and moist his middle!
My dreams, I fear, are infanticiddle.
A fig for embryo Lohengrins!
I'll open all of his safety pins,
I'll pepper his powder, and salt his bottle,
And give him readings from Aristotle.
Sand for his spinach I'll gladly bring,
And Tabasco sauce for his teething ring,
And an elegant, gluttonous alligator
To play with in his perambulator.
Then perhaps he'll struggle through fire and wate.
T* marry somebody else's daughter.

Genealogical Reflection

No McTavish
Was ever lavish.

Ask Daddy, He Won't Know

Now that they've abolished chrome work
    I'd like to call their attention to home work.
Here it is only three decades since my scholarship was
    famous,
And I'm an ignoramus.
I cannot think which goes sideways and which goes up
    and down, a parallel or a meridian,
Nor do I know the name of him who first translated the
    Bible into Indian, I see him only as an enterprising
    colonial Gideon.
I have difficulty with dates,
To say nothing of the annual rainfall of the Southern
    Central States,
And the only way I can distinguish proper from im-
    proper fractions
Is by their actions.
Naturally the correct answers are just back of the tip of
    my tongue,
But try to explain that to your young.
I am overwhelmed by their erudite banter,
I am in no condition to differentiate between Timo-
    shenko and Tam o'Shanter.
I reel, I sway, I am utterly exhausted;
Should you ask me when Chicago was founded I could
    only reply I didn't even know it was losted.

When You Say That, Smile!
or
All Right Then, Don't Smile

WHEN the odds are long,
   And the game goes wrong,
Does your *joie de vivre* diminish?
Have you little delight
In an uphill fight?
Do you wince at a Garrison finish?
Then here's my hand, my trusty partner!
I've always wanted a good disheartener.

Oh, things are frequently what they seem,
And this is wisdom's crown:
Only the game fish swims upstream,
But the sensible fish swims down.

Well, how is your pulse
When a cad insults
The lady you're cavaliering?
Are you willing to wait
To retaliate
Till the cad is out of hearing?
Then here's my hand, my trusty companion,
And may neither one of us fall in a canyon.

For things are frequently what they seem,
And this is wisdom's crown:
Only the game fish swims upstream,
But the sensible fish swims down.

The Rhinoceros

THE rhino is a homely beast,
　For human eyes he's not a feast.
Farewell, farewell, you old rhinoceros,
I'll stare at something less prepoceros.

I Had No Idea It Was So Late

CONSIDER the man without a watch.
　He is like a soda without Scotch.
Of the male character I can quickly give you the gist;
It is the reach for the pocket or the glance at the wrist.
From the moment they are fledglings
Males discipline themselves with timings and schedul
　　ings.
Be they lovers, golfers, or railroad engineers,
Time is the essential ingredient in their careers,
And there is nothing more surly
Than a watchless man who doesn't know whether he is
　　late or early,
And clocks are no good to him because he can't take
　　them along,
And anyhow a clock is only something that you compare
　　with your watch and find the clock is several min-
　　utes wrong.

If there is one thing that every man thinks how sublime
it is,
It is to know what time it is.
Women don't like watches, they only tolerate them when
they are embedded in brooches or bracelets or belts,
Or in some way disguised to look like something else.
Yes, it's obvious that women don't like them or need
them,
Because with women's watches you need a microscope
and a map to read them.
Time is something they resent, and they fight it with
peculiarly feminine resistance;
They refuse to acknowledge its existence.
In this sexual conflict in attitude toward time who am I
to tip the scales?
I only know that more males wait for females than fe-
males wait for males.

A *Plea for Less Malice Toward None*

Love is a word that is constantly heard,
    Hate is a word that's not.
Love, I am told, is more precious than gold,
Love, I have read, is hot.
But hate is the verb that to me is superb,
And love is a drug on the mart.
Any kiddie in school can love like a fool,
But hating, my boy, is an art.

Oh, you and I and many others
Love our sweethearts and our mothers,
Love our spouses, love our tots,
Ship our love in carload lots—
Parsley, parsnips, Golden Buck,
Baked Alaska, Bombay Duck,
Sunup, sundown, sunray lamps,
Sporting prints or postage stamps,
Persimmons, even good persimmons,
Lifted faces, fallen womens,
Woes of Little Orphan Annie
Merry japes about the fanny—
Not a topic named above
That countless millions do not love.
Something somewhere's bound to pop.
I for one suggest we stop.

Hate is a word that is given the bird,
Love is the word that's lauded.

Hate, people say, is completely passé,
Vulgar, my dear, and saudid.
The atmosphere swoons with amorous tunes,
Like turtle dove calling to dove.
We are fairly discreet about what we eat,
But boy! are we gluttons in love!

Oh, fellow countrymen and others,
Turn, I beg, upon your mothers.
No more nonsense from your tots;
Teach them early what are whats.
Learn, before it grows too late,
Fellow countrymen, to hate.
Learn to hate banana salads,
Travel movies, cowboy ballads,
Literati, early risers,
Office-holders, advertisers,
Fruit-juice cocktails, borrowed wit,
Ladies who rely on It;
And fall, I pray on yonder crooner,
Stuff his mouth with goona-goona.
Develop all your latent phobias,
And heaven's blessings will be copious.

Reflection on Caution

AFFECTION is a noble quality;
    It leads to generosity and jollity.
But it also leads to breach of promise
If you go around lavishing it on red-hot momise

Don't Guess, Let Me Tell You

PERSONALLY I don't care whether a detective story
    writer was educated in night school or day school
So long as they don't belong to the H.I.B.K. school.
The H.I.B.K. being a device to which too many detective
    story writers are prone,
Namely the Had I But Known.
Sometimes it is the Had I But Known what grim secret
    lurked behind that smiling exterior I would never
    have set foot within the door,
Sometimes the Had I But Known then what I know now
    I could have saved at least three lives by revealing
    to the Inspector the conversation I heard through
    that fortuitous hole in the floor.
Had-I-But-Known narrators are the ones who hear a
    stealthy creak at midnight in the tower where the
    body lies, and, instead of locking their door or arous-
    ing the drowsy policeman posted outside their room,

sneak off by themselves to the tower and suddenly
they hear a breath exhaled behind them,

And they have no time to scream, they know nothing
else till the men from the D.A.'s office come in next
morning and find them.

Had I But Known-ers are quick to assume the preroga-
tives of the Deity,

For they will suppress evidence that doesn't suit their
theories with appalling spontaneity,

And when the killer is finally trapped into a confession
by some elaborate device of the Had I But Known-er
some hundred pages later than if they hadn't held
their knowledge aloof,

Why they say Why Inspector I knew all along it was he
but I couldn't tell you, you would have laughed at
me unless I had absolute proof.

Would you like a nice detective story for your library
which I am sorry to say I didn't rent but owns?

I wouldn't have bought it had I but known it was im-
pregnated with Had I But Knowns.

Taboo to Boot

ONE bliss for which
    There is no match
Is, when you itch,
To up and scratch.

Yet doctors and dowagers deprecate scratching,
Society ranks it with spitting and snatching,
And medical circles consistently hold
That scratching's as wicked as feeding a cold.
Hell's flame burns unquenched 'neath how many a stock
    ing
On account of to scratch in a salon is shocking!
Avid ankles deprived of the fingernail's kiss
For fear of a dermatological hiss!

    'Neath tile or thatch
    That man is rich
    Who has a scratch
    For every itch.

Ho, squirmers and writhers, how long will ye suffer
The medical tyrant, the social rebuffer!
On the edge of the door let our shoulder blades rub,
Let the drawing room now be as free as the tub!
Let us scratch in the presence of multitudes medical
And if they object, let us call them unedical!
So the ogres of ivy and ringworm and allergies
We'll scratch to the stature of abject apologies!

I'm greatly attached
To Barbara Frietchie.
I bet she scratched
When she was itchy.

The Fish

THE fish, when he's exposed to air,
    Displays no trace of savoir faire,
But in the sea regains his balance
And exploits all his manly talents.
The chastest of the vertebrates,
He never even sees his mates,
But when they've finished, he appears
And O.K.'s all their bright ideas.

Mr. Peachey's Predicament
or
No Mot Parades

ONCE there was a man named Mr. Peachey and he
lived on Park Avenue and played the harp and was
an eligible bachelor but his social life was hapless,

And he thought at first it was because his parents came
from Indianapless,

But one day he awoke from a troubled nap,

And said I am tired of this hapless social life, what I
want is a social life simply teeming with hap.

It can't be, he said, that I don't play the harp enough,

I wonder if just possibly my wits are not sharp enough.

I know that I'm pretty noted

But I've never been quoted;

Perhaps the solution for me

Is some iridescent repartee;

Suppose before I next dine out I compose a series of epigrams of searing astringency

And then I shall be ready with a quip for any conversa-
tional contingency.

So he composed a series of epigrams of indubitable
variety,

And went to dine with some people way up in society.

And in the taxi he memorized his lines and held a solo
rehearsal,

And he was delighted, because he said some people's
humor is specialized but mine is universal.

There may well be a Mr. Shoemaker there who has
    divorced a beautiful rich virtuous wife for a debt-
    ridden hideous wife with a past,
And I'll say Shoemaker you should have stuck to your last;
And suppose somebody remarks that the hostess looks
    like a Titian I can bring them up short,
I can answer, Looks like a Titian, eh? Do you mean
    beaut- or mort-?
And I'll go right on and say While we're on the subject
    of waltzes I'd like to play a little Haydn for you, and
    I'll go to the piano and grope at the keys and then
    look up impishly and speak,
And say I really don't know whether I'm playing Haydn
    or Haydn seek.
Then after the laughter has died down I shall approach
    some Yale man who has just returned from abroad
    whom I wish to embarrass
And I'll ask him how he enjoyed the Boola-Boolavards of
    Paris.
Oh, said Mr. Peachey gleefully, the days of my hapless
    social life are over, I cannot help but be a wow,
I wish I was at the party right now.
But when he got to the party his hostess, who didn't look like
    a Titian at all, she looked like a Dali, was quite sharp,
And sent him right back to his Park Avenue apartment
    to get his harp,
And today he is living in the old family mansion in In-
    dianapless
Where I'm sorry to say his social life is just as hapless.

Some of My Best Friends Are Children

ICHNEUMONS are fond of little ichneumons,
  And lions of little lions,
But I am not fond of little humans;
I do not believe in scions.

Of course there's always our child,
But our child is different,
Our child appeals
To the cultivated mind.
Ours is a lady;
Boys are odoriferant;
Ladies are the sweetness;
Boys are the rind.

Whenever whimsy collides with whimsy
As parents compare their cherubs,
At the slightest excuse, however flimsy,
I fold my tent like the Arabs.

Of course there's always our child,
But our child is charminger,
Our child's eyes
Are a special kind of blue;
Our child's smile
Is quite a lot disarminger;
Our child's tooth
Is very nearly through.

Mankind, I consider, attained its zenith
The day it achieved the adult;
When the conversation to infants leaneth,
My horse is bridled and saddult.

Of course there's always our child,
But our child is wittier;
Our child's noises
Are the nicest kind of noise;
She has no beard
Like Tennyson or Whittier;
But Tennyson and Whittier
Began as little boys.

The Politician, the Parent, the Preacher,
Were each of them once a kiddie.
The child is indeed a talented creature.
Do I want one? Oh God forbidde!

Of course there's always our child
But our child's adorable.
Our child's an angel
Fairer than the flowers;
Our child fascinates
One who's rather borable;
And incidentally,
Our child is ours.

The Turtle

THE turtle lives 'twixt plated decks
    Which practically conceal its sex.
I think it clever of the turtle
In such a fix to be so fertile.

Don't Look Now

THERE is something to be said for the Victorians
    Even though they refused to believe they were
        descended from apes and saurians;
Because take their low opinion of exposure anatomical,
Why I have a feeling that they felt it was not so much
    immoral as just plain comical.
They realized that most people are big where they
    should be littler and little where they should be
    bigger,
And they would rather have had their bathing suit
    laughed at than their figure.
Yes they wore the costumes they did because they knew
    that they were not ancient Greeks,
And it is a moot question which is more ludicrous on the
    beach, the cloistered rompers of the nineties, or to-
    day's ubiquitous physiques.
The belle of the nineties tiptoeing down the steps of the

bathing machine may have had the natural lines of a Langtry or again of a prize-winning pumpkin or of a homeless heifer after an extended drought,

But thanks to the marquee enswathing her she got the benefit of the doubt.

Whereas today at Miami or Coney or Catalina,

Why practically everyone is forced to face the fact that their beloved is built like either a flute or a concertina.

I have a theory about physiological disclosures along the strand;

I believe they account for Sally Rand;

I believe that when people have seen a certain number of undraped figures like a concertina or a flute,

Well, finally they are willing to pay any amount just to see a beaut,

So now it's a hot sultry day and you may all run down to the beach for a swim and a look.

I'm going to put on Uncle Elmer's bathing suit and sit in the tub and read a Victorian book.

Nevertheless

I AM not fond of Oliver Montrose.
   Oliver is a person I despise;
The purple veins that bulbify his nose,
The crimson veins that irrigate his eyes.
His wheezy breath his vinous weakness shows;
He is the slave of whisky, beer and gin.
I am not fond of Oliver Montrose;
I hate the sinner. But what a warming sin!

Bibesco Poolidge is a man of jowl;
I've never seen a dewlap, but on him;
He shines with the grease of many a basted fowl;
Ten thousand sauces round his innards swim.
The ghosts of hosts of kine about him prowl,
Lamb, pig, and game blood trickles from his chin;
I cannot look on him without a scowl;
I hate the sinner. But what a luscious sin!

I do not dote on Murgatroyd Van Rust,
So tasty to the tenderest of genders.
Practically everything that has a bust
Surveys his suave ensemble and surrenders.
The way he parts his hair I do not trust;
Let the phone ring, I loathe his knowing grin.
You cannot see his diary for the dust,
I hate the sinner. Still, if one *had* to sin . . .

O Mammonites and spendthrifts, draw ye nigh,
Fingernail-biters and sluggards, come on in,
Consider now how tolerant am I
Who hate the sinner, yet who love the sin.

Reflection on the Passage of Time, Its Inevitability and Its Quirks

IN NINETEEN hunderd
    Jeunes filles wondered.

Two and One Are a Problem

DEAR Miss Dix, I am a young man of half-past thirty-seven.

My friends say I am not unattractive, though to be kind and true is what I have always striven.

I am open-minded about beverages so long as they are grape, brandy or malt,

And I am generous to practically any fault.

Well Miss Dix not to beat around the bush, there is a certain someone who thinks I am pretty nice,

And I turn to you for advice.

You see, it started when I was away on the road

And returned to find a pair of lovebirds had taken up their residence in my abode.

Well I am not crazy about lovebirds, but I must say they looked very sweet in their gilded cage,

And their friendship had reached an advanced stage,

And I had just forgiven her who of the feathered fiancés
    was the donor of

When the houseboy caught a lost lovebird in the yard
    that we couldn't locate the owner of.

So then we had three, and it was no time for flippancy,

Because everybody knows that a lovebird without its
    own lovebird to love will pine away and die of the
    discrepancy,

So we bought a fourth lovebird for the third lovebird
    and they sat around very cozily beak to beak

And then the third lovebird that we had provided the
    fourth lovebird for to keep it from dying died at the
    end of the week,

So we were left with an odd lovebird and it was no time
    for flippancy,

Because a lovebird without its own lovebird to love will
    pine away and die of the discrepancy,

So we had to buy a fifth lovebird to console the fourth
    lovebird that we had bought to keep the third love-
    bird contented,

And now the fourth lovebird has lost its appetite, and,
    Miss Dix, I am going demented.

I don't want to break any hearts, but I got to know
    where I'm at;

Must I keep on buying lovebirds, Miss Dix, or do you
    think it would be all right to buy a cat?

One Third of a Calendar

IN JANUARY everything freezes.
   We have two children. Both are she'ses.
This is our January rule:
One girl in bed, and one in school.

In February the blizzard whirls.
We own a pair of little girls.
Blessings upon of each the head—
The one in school and the one in bed.

March is the month of cringe and bluster.
Each of our children has a sister.
They cling together like Hansel and Gretel,
With their noses glued to the benzoin kettle.

April is made of impetuous waters
And doctors looking down throats of daughters.
If we had a son too, and a Samoyed,
We'd have a dog,
And a boy,
And two girls
In bed.

Song of the Open Road

I THINK that I shall never see
    A billboard lovely as a tree.
Indeed, unless the billboards fall
I'll never see a tree at all.

Good-bye, Old Year, You Oaf,
or
Why Don't They Pay the Bonus?

MANY of the three hundred and sixty-five days of the
year are followed by dreadful nights but one
night is by far, oh yes, by far the worst, .

And that, my friends, is the night of December the
thirty-first.

Man can never get it through his head that he is born
to be not a creditor but a debtor;

Man always thinks the annual thought that just because
last year was terrible next year is bound to be better.

Man is a victim of dope

In the incurable form of hope;

Man is a blemishless Pollyanna,

And is convinced that the advent of every New Year
will place him in possession of a bumper crop of
manna.

Therefore Man fills himself up with a lot of *joie de vivre*

And goes out to celebrate New Year's *Ivre*;

Therefore millions of respectable citizens who just a
week before have been perfectly happy to sit at
home and be cosily Christmas carolized

Consider it a point of honor to go out on the town and
get themselves paralyzed;

Therefore the whistles blow toot toot and the bells ring
ding ding and the confetti goes confetti confetti at
midnight on the thirty-first of December,

And on January first the world is full of people who
either can't and wish they could, or can and wish
they couldn't remember.
They never seem to learn from experience;
They keep on doing it year after year from the time they
are puling infants till they are doddering octoge-
nerience.
My goodness, if there's anything in heredity and en-
vironment
How can people expect the new-born year to manifest
any culture or refironment?
Every new year is the direct descendant, isn't it, of a
long line of proven criminals?
And you can't turn it into a philanthropist by welcoming
it with cocktails and champagne any more success-
fully than with prayer books and hyminals.
Every new year is a country as barren as the old one,
and it's no use trying to forage it;
Every new year is incorrigible, then all I can say is for
Heaven's sakes, why go out of your way to incorrage
it?

Geddondillo

THE sharrot scudders nights in the quastron now,
  The dorlim slinks undeceded in the grost,
Appetency lights the corb of the guzzard now,
The ancient beveldric is otley lost.

Treduty flees like a darbit along the drace now,
Collody lollops belutedly over the slawn.
The bloodbound bitterlitch bays the ostrous moon now,
For yesterday's bayable majicity is flunkly gone.

Make way, make way, the preluge is scarly nonce now,
Make way, I say, the gronderous Demiburge comes,
His blidless veins shall ye joicily rejugulate now,
And gollify him from 'twixt his protecherous gums.

Platitudinous Reflection

A GOOD deal of superciliousness
   Is based on biliousness.
People seem to be proud as peacocks
Of any infirmity, be it hives or dementia praecox.

What's the Matter, Haven't You Got Any Sense of Humor?

THERE is at least one thing I would less rather have in the neighborhood than a gangster,

And that one thing is a practical prankster.

I feel that we should differ more sharply than Montagues and Capulets or York and Lancaster,

Me and a practical prancaster.

If there is a concentration camp in limbo, that is the spot for which I nominate them,

Not because I don't like them, but simply because I abominate them.

The born practical prankster starts out in early youth by offering people a chair,

And when they sit down it isn't there,

And he is delighted and proceeds to more complicated wheezes,

Such as ten cent X-rays to see through people's clothes with and powders to give them itches and sneezes,

And his boutonniere is something that people get squirted in the eye out of,

And their beds are what he makes apple pie out of.

Then as he matures he widens his scope,

And he is no longer content to present people with exploding cigars and chocolate creams with centers of soap,

So he dresses up as an Oriental potentate and reviews the British fleet,

Or collects a little group of kinsprits and a few pick-
    axes and a STREET CLOSED sign and digs up a
    busy street,
And if people are jumpy about their past or present
    private lives he hints that he is writing his memoirs
    and is devoting an entire chapter to their particular
    skeleton,
And finally he reaches the apex of his career when he
    slips into somebody's bathroom and fills up all the
    modern conveniences with water and then adds
    raspberry gelatin.
I have recently read with complete satisfaction of a
    practical prankster two of whose friends had just
    been married,
Which was of course in itself simply a challenge to be
    harried,
And it was a challenge he was eager to meet,
And he went to the roof of their hotel and tied a rope
    around his waist and a colleague lowered him to
    where he could clash a pair of cymbals outside the
    window of the nuptial suite,
And he weighed two hundred and eighty pounds and
    the rope broke,
And that to my mind is the perfect practical joke.

Tin Wedding Whistle

THOUGH you know it anyhow,
Listen to me, darling, now,

Proving what I need not prove
How I know I love you, love.

Near and far, near and far,
I am happy where you are;

Likewise I have never larnt
How to be it where you aren't.

Far and wide, far and wide,
I can walk with you beside;

Furthermore, I tell you what,
I sit and sulk where you are not.

Visitors remark my frown
When you're upstairs and I am down,

Yes, and I'm afraid I pout
When I'm indoors and you are out;

But how contentedly I view
Any room containing you.

In fact I care not where you be,
Just as long as it's with me.

In all your absences I glimpse
Fire and flood and trolls and imps.

Is your train a minute slothful?
I goad the stationmaster wrothful.

When with friends to bridge you drive
I never know if you're alive,

And when you linger late in shops
I long to telephone the cops.

Yet how worth the waiting for,
To see you coming through the door.

Somehow, I can be complacent
Never but with you adjacent.

Near and far, near and far,
I am happy where you are;

Likewise, I have never larnt
How to be it where you aren't.

Then grudge me not my fond endeavor,
To hold you in my sight forever;

Let none, not even you, disparage
Such valid reason for a marriage.

These Latins

THE bashful Spaniardess apparently finds the amorous Spaniard so menacing to her virtue
That she has to employ a duenna so that he shan't duennacing to her virtue.

Mr. Artesian's Conscientiousness

ONCE there was a man named Mr. Artesian and his
   activity was tremendous,
And he grudged every minute away from his desk because the importance of his work was so stupendous;
And he had one object all sublime,
Which was to save simply oodles of time.
He figured that sleeping eight hours a night meant that
   if he lived to be seventy-five he would have spent
   twenty-five years not at his desk but in bed,
So he cut his slumber to six hours which meant he only
   lost eighteen years and nine months instead,
And he figured that taking ten minutes for breakfast and
   twenty minutes for luncheon and half an hour for
   dinner meant that he spent three years, two months
   and fifteen days at the table,
So that by subsisting solely on bouillon cubes which he
   swallowed at his desk to save this entire period he
   was able,
And he figured that at ten minutes a day he spent a little
   over six months and ten days shaving,
So he grew a beard, which gave him a considerable
   saving,
And you might think that now he might have been
   satisfied, but no, he wore a thoughtful frown,
Because he figured that at two minutes a day he would
   spend thirty-eight days and a few minutes in elevators just traveling up and down,

So as a final timesaving device he stepped out the window of his office, which happened to be on the fiftieth floor,

And one of his partners asked "Has he vertigo?" and the other glanced out and down and said "Oh no, only about ten feet more."

The Voice of Experience

A HUSBAND at a lecture
   Twitches his architecture.

He undergoes the lecturing
Like unanesthetized vivisecturing.

He's a glassy-eyed conjecturer
Of the ancestry of the lecturer.

Husbands hide in storerooms
To escape Town Halls and Forums.

They improvise In Memoriams
For speakers in auditoriums.

They regard as nauseous nostrums
Opinions delivered from rostrums.

They feel about orators' rhetorics
Like Cæsar about Vercingetorix.

They flinch as the fog of boredom
Creeps verbosely toredom.

Their collars grow more and more cumbersome,
And at last they essay to slumber some.

But this respite their spouses grudge them,
And if they nod, they nudge them.

There is none so irate and awkward
As a husband being Chautauquard.

The Sea-Gull

Hark to the whimper of the sea-gull;
He weeps because he's not an ea-gull.
Suppose you were, you silly sea-gull,
Could you explain it to your she-gull?

Are You a Snodgrass?

IT is possible that most individual and international
social and economic collisions
Result from humanity's being divided into two main
divisions,
Both of which are irreconcilable,
And neither is by the other beguilable;
Their lives are spent in mutual interference,
And yet you cannot tell them apart by their outward
appearance.
Indeed the only way in which to tell one group from the
other you are able
Is to observe them at the table,
Because the only visible way in which one group from
the other varies
Is in its treatment of the cream and sugar on cereal and
berries.
Group A, which we will call the Swozzlers because it is
a very suitable name, I deem,
First applies the sugar and then swozzles it all over the
place pouring on the cream,
And as fast as they put the sugar on they swozzle it
away,
But such thriftlessness means nothing to ruthless egotists
like they,
They just continue to scoop and swozzle and swozzle
and scoop,

Until there is nothing left for the Snodgrasses, or second
group.

A Snodgrass is a kind, handsome, intelligent person who
pours the cream on first,

And then deftly sprinkles the sugar over the cereal or
berries after they have been properly immersed,

Thus assuring himself that the sugar will remain on the
cereal and berries where it can do some good, which
is his wish,

Instead of being swozzled away to the bottom of the
dish.

The facts of the case for the Snodgrasses are so self-
evident that it is ridiculous to debate them,

But this is unfortunate for the Snodgrasses as it only
causes the sinister and vengeful Swozzlers all the
more to hate them.

Swozzlers are irked by the superior Snodgrass intelli-
gence and nobility

And they lose no opportunity of inflicting on them every
kind of incivility.

If you read that somebody has been run over by an
automobile

You may be sure that the victim was a Snodgrass, and a
Swozzler was at the wheel.

Swozzlers start wars and Snodgrasses get killed in them,

Swozzlers sell water-front lots and Snodgrasses get ma-
laria when they try to build in them.

Swozzlers invent fashionable diets and drive Snodgrasses crazy with tables of vitamins and calories,

Swozzlers go to Congress and think up new taxes and
     Snodgrasses pay their salaries,
Swozzlers bring tigers back alive and Snodgrasses get
     eaten by anacondas,
Snodgrasses are depositors and Swozzlers are absconders,
Swozzlers hold straight flushes when Snodgrasses hold
     four of a kind,
Swozzlers step heavily on the toes of Snodgrass's shoes
     as soon as they are shined.
Whatever achievements Snodgrasses achieve, Swozzlers
     always top them;
Snodgrasses say Stop me if you've heard this one, and
     Swozzlers stop them.
Swozzlers are teeming with useful tricks of the trade
     that are not included in standard university cur-
     ricula;
The world in general is their oyster, and Snodgrasses in
     particular.
So I hope for your sake, dear reader, that you are a
     Swozzler, but I hope for everybody else's sake that
     you are not,
And I also wish that everybody else was a nice amiable
     Snodgrass too, because then life would be just one
     long sweet harmonious mazurka or gavotte.

Old Men

PEOPLE expect old men to die,
   They do not really mourn old men.
Old men are different. People look
At them with eyes that wonder when . . .
People watch with unshocked eyes . . .
But the old men know when an old man dies.

Birdies, Don't Make Me Laugh

ONCE there was a poem, and it wasn't by Edgar A. Guest,

And it said children ought to agree like little birdies in their nest.

Oh forsooth forsooth!

That poem was certainly more poetry than truth,

Because do you believe that little birdies in their nest agree?

It doesn't sound very probable to me.

Ah no, but I can tell you what does sound probable,

And that is that life in a nest is just one long quarrel and squabbable.

Look at that young mother robin over in that elm, or is it a beech,

She has two little robins and she thinks she has solved her problem because she has learned not to bring home just one worm but a worm for each.

She is very pleased with her understanding of fledgling psychology, but in just about two minutes she is going to lose a year's growth,

Because she's going to find that one little robin gets no worms and the other little robin gets both,

And if one little robin gets out of the nest on the wrong side and nothing can please it,

Why the other little robin will choose that moment to tease it,

And if one little robin starts a game the other little robin
 will stop it,
And if one little robin builds a castle the other little
 robin will knock it down and if one little robin blows
 a bubble the other little robin will pop it.
Yes, I bet that if you walked up to any nest and got a
 good revealing glimpse,
Why, you would find that our little feathered friendlets
 disagree just like human imps,
And I also bet that their distracted feathered parents
 quote feathered poetry to them by whoever the most
 popular feathered poet may be,
All about why don't they like little children in their
 nurseries agree.
Well, to put the truth about youth in a very few words,
Why the truth is that little birds do agree like children
 and children do agree like little birds,
Because you take offspring, and I don't care whether a
 house or a tree is their abode,
They may love each other but they aren't going to agree
 with each other anywhere except in an ode.
It doesn't seem to have occurred to the poet,
That nobody agrees with anybody else anyhow. but
 adults conceal it and infants show it.

Electra Becomes Morbid

I

ABANDON for a moment, friends,
   Your frivolous means, your futile ends;
Life is not wholly beer and skittles,
A treasure hunt for love and victuals;
And so at times I think we ought
To pause and think a sobering thought.
Myself, I feel a dark despair
When I consider human hair.
I'm chicken-hearted, beetle-browed,
As I behold the heedless crowd,
Knowing each carefree individual
The slave of hair that runs on schidual.
On every human head or chin
It's falling out or growing in.
Yon whistling adolescent scholar,
Released from Ye Olde Tonsorial Parlor,
Runs up his neck with fingers tense
Like sticks along a picket fence.
His scalp is all Bay Rum and bristles,
Therefore he's pleased and therefore whistles.
Yea, he rejoices, quite unknowing
That all the time his hair is growing.
O woe is you, unhappy scholar,
Next month you'll be back in the tonsorial parlor

Myself I feel a dark despair,
When I consider human hair
(Fine filaments sprouting from the skin),
I tremble like an aspirin.
For men and women everywhere
Unconsciously are growing hair,
Or, if the other hand you choose,
With every breath a hair they lose.
Unbid it cometh, likewise goeth,
And oftentimes it's doing boeth.
This habit is the chief determinant
Why permanent waves are less than permanent.
You rise, Madame, you face your mirror,
You utter cries of shame and terror.
What though to males you look all right?
For heaven's sake, your hair's a sight.
You hasten to the Gallic lair
Where lurks Maurice, or Jean or Pierre.
Between arrival and departure
You suffer hours of vicious torture,
At last emerging, white and weak,
But sure at least your mane is chic.
Thus you rejoice, my dear, unknowing
That all the time your hair is growing.
The waves so dearly purchased
Next month will have grown a foot or so away from
    your head.

I've said, I think, I think we ought
To think at times a sobering thought.
Man's lot it is to be a field
For crops that no nutrition yield,
That filter through his tender skin
And ripen on his head or chin.
I face mankind and shudder, knowing
That everybody's hair is growing;
That lovers, linked in darkened hallways,
Are capped with hair that groweth always;
That millions, shaven in the morning,
At eve find beards their jowls adorning;
That hair is creeping through the scalps
Of yodelers yodeling in the Alps,
And pushing through the epidermises
Of peasants frolicking at kermises;
And poking bravely through the pores
Of cannibals on tropic shores;
That freezing, scorching, raining, snowing,
People's hair is always growing.
I contemplate with dark despair
The awful force of growing hair,
Although admitting, to be quite honest,
That it will be worth a million Niagaras to humanity if
    Science can ever get it harnessed.

The Rooster

THE rooster has a soul more bellicose
    Than all your Ludendorffs and Jellicoes.
His step is prouder than Davy Crockett's,
As he swaggers by with his hands in his pockets.

Look for the Silver Lining

I CAN'T say that I feel particularly one way or the other
    towards bell-boys,
But I do admit that I haven't much use for the it's-just-
    as-well boys,
The cheery souls who drop around after every catastro-
    phe and think they are taking the curse off
By telling you about somebody who is even worse off.
No matter how deep and dark your pit, how dank your
    shroud,
Their heads are heroically unbloody and unbowed.
If you have just lost the one love of your life, there is no
    possible doubt of it,
They tell you there are as good fish in the sea as ever
    came out of it.
If you are fined ten dollars for running past a light when
    you didn't but the cop says you did,
They say Cheer up think of the thousand times you ran
    past them and didn't get caught so you're really ten
    thousand bucks ahead, Hey old kid?
If you lose your job they tell you how lucky you are that
    you've saved up a little wealth
And then when the bank folds with the savings they tell
    you you sure are lucky to still have your health.
Life to them is just one long happy game,
At the conclusion of which the One Great Scorer writes
    not whether you won it or lost it, but how you
    played it, against your name.

Kismet, they say, it's Fate. What is to be, will be. Buck
up! Take heart!

Kismet indeed! Nobody can make me grateful for Paris
Green in the soup just by assuring me that it comes
that way Allah carte.

In Which the Poet Is Ashamed but Pleased

OF ALL the things that I would rather,
It is to be my daughter's father,
While she, with innocence divine,
Is quite contented to be mine.

I am distressingly aware
That this arrangement is unfair,
For I, when in my celibate garrison,
Acquired some standard of comparison.

I visited nurseries galore,
Compiled statistics by the score,
And gained experience from a crew
Of children passing in review.

And some were fair and some were dark
And some were clothed and some were stark,
And some were howling, teasing demons,
And some as sweet as Mrs. Hemans.

I saw the best that parents vaunted;
They weren't exactly what I wanted;
Yet, all the offspring that I faced,
They served to cultivate my taste.

Thus, let the miser praise the mintage,
And let the vintner praise the vintage;

I'm conscious that in praising her,
I'm speaking as a connoisseur.

While she, poor dear, has never known
A father other than her own.
She wots of other girls' papas
No more than of the Persian Shah's.

Within her head no notion stirs
That some are better men than hers;
That some are richer, some are kinder,
Some are solider, some refineder,

That some are vastly more amusing
Some fitter subjects for enthusing,
That some are cleverer, some are braver,
Than the one that fortune gave her.

What fortune set us side by side,
Her scope so narrow, mine so wide?
We owe to this sweet dispensation
Our mutual appreciation.

The Panther

THE panther is like a leopard,
   Except it hasn't been peppered.
Should you behold a panther crouch,
Prepare to say Ouch.
Better yet, if called by a panther,
Don't anther.

Watchman, What of the First First Lady?

Everybody can tell you the date of George Washington's birth,

But who knows the date on which Mrs. George Washington first appeared on earth?

Isn't there any justice

For the former Mrs. Custis?

Of course her memory is perpetuated by a hotel,

But Hell.

It's a disgrace to every United State

That we don't know more about our first president's only mate.

We all know a lot of stories about the wife of King Arthur

But you never hear any about Martha,

And we have all read a lot of romantic tales about Catherine the Great,

But nobody ever writes them about Washington's mate,

And we have all seen Katharine Cornell, or was it Helen Hayes or Ethel Barrymore,

Impersonate Cleopatra, who wasn't even anybody's real wife but nothing more or less than a promiscuous un-American parrymore,

But has anybody done anything about the mistress of the nation's whitest house?

No, and yet but for her the nation would be the child of a man without a spouse.

Please Pass the Biscuit

I HAVE a little dog,
Her name is Spangle.
And when she eats
I think she'll strangle.

She's darker than Hamlet,
Lighter than Porgy;
Her heart is gold,
Her odor, dorgy.

Her claws click-click
Across the floor,
Her nose is always
Against a door.

The squirrel flies
Her pursuing mouth;
Should he fly north,
She pursues him south.

Yet do not mock her
As she hunts;
Remember, she caught
A milkman once.

Like liquid gems
Her eyes burn clearly;

She's five years old,
And house-trained, nearly.

Her shame is deep
When she has erred;
She dreads the blow
Less than the word.

I marvel that such
Small ribs as these
Can cage such vast
Desire to please.

She's as much a part
Of the house as the mortgage;
Spangle, I wish you
A ripe old dortgage.

The Termite

SOME primal termite knocked on wood
And tasted it, and found it good,
And that is why your Cousin May
Fell through the parlor floor today.

From a Manhattan Tomb

I KNOW that a little verse is a versicle but I don't know
    if a little phrase is a phrasicle
But I do know that at the moment I feel too too alas and
    alackadaisicle.
What though around me is the hustle and bustle of a
    great city at its labors?
What though I am hemmed in by the most industrious
    and ingenious kind of neighbors?
What though young people are joining forever or parting
    forever with each tick of the clock?
What though Mr. Belloc admires Mr. Chesterton or Mr.
    Chesterton admires Mr. Belloc?
What though to produce the Sunday papers thousands
    of square miles of Canada are deforested?
What though in an attempt to amuse the public thou-
    sands of writers and actors and things are utterly
    exhorested?
What though young humans are getting born and old
    humans are getting deceased and middle-aged hu-
    mans are getting used to it?
What though a Bronxville husband has discovered that
    he can put the baby to sleep by reading Proust to it?
All these things may be of great moment to those who
    are concerned with them in any way,
But how are they going to help me to get through the
    day?

For I have had to eat luncheon while I was still sorry I
 had eaten breakfast and I shall have to eat dinner
 while I am still sorry I ate luncheon
And my spirit has been put through the third degree
 and thrown into a very dark dank dismal duncheon
Why do people insist on bringing me anecdotes and al
 legories and alcohol and food?
Why won't they just let me sit and brood?
Why does the population swirl around me with viva-
 cious violence
When all I want to do is sit and suffer in siolence?
Everybody I see tries to cheer me up
And I wish they would stop.

The Hat's Got My Tongue

A GIRL, oh a girl is a wonderful thing,
    And so I am happy to say is spring,
And a girl in spring is the absolute works
But for one conspicuous item that irks:
That hat.

A girl in spring is a skylark's hymn,
An evensong in a cloister dim,
A moon in June and a dove in love,
But why the discordant detail above:
That hat?

The crocuses put their best feet foremost,
The softest, tenderest raindrops pour most,
Nature walks forth in a robe of dawn,
And you, my love, what do you put on?
That hat.

Purple the lilac and green the oaks,
Is spring the time for a milliner's hoax?
Your taste, methought, simply hibernated;
But what did I get when for spring I waited?
That hat.

A girl, oh a girl is a wonderful thing,
And so I am happy to say is spring,

And you are what I adore the sight of;
That hat is what I adore you in spite of—
Take it off and let's jump on it!

The Fly

G OD in His wisdom made the fly,
And then forgot to tell us why.

Lines to a World-Famous Poet Who Failed
to Complete a World-Famous Poem
or
Come Clean, Mr. Guest!

O FT when I'm sitting without anything to read waiting for a train in a depot,
I torment myself with the poet's dictum that to make a
house a home, livin' is what it takes a heap o'.
Now, I myself should very much enjoy makin' my house
a home, but my brain keeps on a-goin' clickety-
click, clickety-click, clickety-click,
If Peter Piper picked a peck o' heap o' livin', what kind
of a peck o' heap o' livin' would Peter Piper pick?
Certainly a person doesn't need the brains of a Lincoln
To know that there are many kinds o' livin', just as there
are many kinds o' dancin' or huntin' or fishin' or
eatin' or drinkin'.
A philosophical poet should be specific
As well as prolific,
And I trust I am not being offensive

If I suggest that he should also be comprehensive.

You may if you like verify my next statement by sending a stamped, self-addressed envelope to either Dean Inge or Dean Gauss,

But meanwhile I ask you to believe that it takes a heap of other things besides a heap o' livin' to make a home out of a house.

To begin with, it takes a heap o' payin',

And you don't pay just the oncet, but agayin and agayin and agayin.

Buyin' a stock is called speculatin' and buyin' a house is called investin',

But the value of the stock or of the house fluctuates up and down, generally down, just as an irresponsible Destiny may destine.

Something else that your house takes a heap o', whether the builder came from Sicily or Erin,

Is repairin',

In addition to which, gentle reader, I am sorry to say you are little more than an imbecile or a cretin

If you think it doesn't take a heap o' heatin',

And unless you're spiritually allied to the little Dutch boy who went around inspectin' dikes lookin' for leaks to put his thumb in,

It takes a heap o' plumbin',

And if it's a house that you're hopin' to spend not just today but tomorrow in,

It takes a heap o' borrowin'.

In a word, Macushla,

There's a scad o' things that to make a house a home it takes not only a heap, or a peck, but at least a **bushela.**

The Sniffle

IN SPITE of her sniffle,
  Isabel's chiffle.
Some girls with a sniffle
Would be weepy and tiffle;
They would look awful,
Like a rained-on waffle,
But Isabel's chiffle
In spite of her sniffle.
Her nose is more red
With a cold in her head,
But then, to be sure,
Her eyes are bluer.
Some girls with a snuffle,
Their tempers are uffle,
But when Isabel's snivelly
She's snivelly civilly,
And when she is snuffly
She's perfectly luffly.

Samson Agonistes

I TEST my bath before I sit,
  And I'm always moved to wonderment
That what chills the finger not a bit
Is so frigid upon the fundament.

Oh, Stop Being Thankful All Over the Place

IN THE glittering collection of paste diamonds one in
  particular ranks very high,
And that is the often-quoted remark of the prominent
  and respectable dignitary who on seeing a con-
  demned man on his way to the scaffold crashed into
  a thousand anthologies by remarking, There but for
  the grace of God go I.
Here is a deplorable illustration
Of sloppy ratiocination;
Here is a notable feat
Of one-way thinking on a two-way street.
It must certainly have been the speaker's lucky day,
Or otherwise he would have been run over by his speech
  turning around and coming back the other way,
Because did he stop to work out his premise to its logical
  conclusion? Ah no,
He just got it off and let it go,

And now whenever people are with people they want to
    impress with their combined greatheartedness and
    book-learning they cry
Oh look at that condemned man on his way to the scaf-
    fold, there but for the grace of God go I.
Which is so far so good, but they neglect to continue
    with the heretofore unspoken balance of the theme,
    which is equally true,
That there but for the grace of God goes Jimmie Durante
    or the Prince of Wales or Aimee Semple McPherson
    or Dr. Wellington Koo,
Or Moses or Napoleon or Cleopatra or King Midas,
Or a man named Harris who is just getting over an at-
    tack of tonsilidas.
So away with you, all you parrot-like repeaters of high-
    sounding phrases that you never stop to consider
    what they actually mean,
I wouldn't allow you to stay in any college of which I
    was the Dean.
I can never listen to you without thinking Ob my,
There but for the grace of God speak I.

Dance Unmacabre

This is the witching hour of noon;
  Bedlam breaks upon us soon.
When the stroke of twelve has tolled
What a pageant doth unfold.
Drawers slam on pads of notes,
Eager fingers clutch at coats;
Compact, lipstick, comb and hat,
Here a dab and there a pat;
The vital letter just begun
Can sulk in the machine till one.
Stenographers on clicking heels
Scurry forth in quest of meals;
Secretaries arm in arm
Fill the corridors with charm;
The stolid air with scent grows heavy
As bevy scuttles after bevy;
Like the pipers on the beach,
Calling shrilly each to each,
Sure as arrows, swift as skaters,
Converging at the elevators.
From the crowded lift they scatter
Bursting still with turbulent chatter;
The revolving door in rapture whirls,
Its quarters full of pretty girls.
Soignée, comme il faut and *chic*
On ten to seventeen a week.

When One upon the dial looms
They hurry to their office tombs,
There to bide in dust till five,
When they come again alive.

WHY does the Pygmy
  Indulge in polygmy?
His tribal dogma
Frowns on monogma.
Monogma's a stigma
For any Pygma.
If he sticks to monogmy
A Pygmy's a hogmy.

Suppose I Darken Your Door

IT SEEMS to me that if you must be sociable it is better
   to go and see people than to have people come and
   see you,
Because then you can leave when you are through.
Yes, the moment you begin to nod
You can look at your watch and exclaim Goodness gracious, it is ten o'clock already, I had no idea it was
   so late, how very odd!
And you politely explain that you have to get up early in
   the morning to keep an important engagement with
   a man from Alaska or Siam,
And you politely thank your host and hostess for the
   lovely time and politely say good night and politely
   scram,
But when you yourself are the home team and the gathering is under your own roof,
You haven't got a Manchurian's chance of being aloof.
If you glance at your watch it is grievous breach of hos-
   pitality and a disgrace,
And if you are caught in the midst of a yawn you have
   to pretend you were making a face and say Come on
   everybody, let's see who can make the funniest face.
Then as the evening wears on you feel more and more
   like an unsuccessful gladiator,
Because all the comfortable places to sit in are being
   sat in by guests and you have to repose on the window sill or the chandelier or the radiator,

And somebody has always brought along a girl who looks like a loaf of raisin bread and doesn't know anybody else in the room,

And you have to go over to the corner where she is moping and try to disperse her gloom,

And finally at last somebody gets up and says they have to get back to the country or back to town again,

And you feebly say Oh it's early, don't go yet, so what do they do but sit down again,

And people that haven't said a word all evening begin to get lively and people that have been lively all evening get their second wind and somebody says Let's all go out in the kitchen and scramble some eggs,

And you have to look at him or her twice before you can convince yourself that anybody who would make a suggestion like that hasn't two heads or three legs,

And by this time the birds are twittering in the trees or looking in the window and saying Boo,

But nobody does anything about it and as far as I know they're all still here, and that's the reason I say that it is better to go and see people than to have people come and see you.

Judgment Day

This is the day, this is the day!
  I knew as soon as the sun's first ray
Crept through the slats of the cot,
And opened the eyes of a tot,
And the tot would rather have slept,
And, therefore, wept.
This is the day that is wrong,
The day when the only song
Is a skirling lamentation
Of continuous indignation,
When the visage is ireful,
The voice, direful,
And the early, pearly teeth
Snick like a sword in the sheath,
When the fists are clenched,
And the cheeks are drenched
In full-fed freshets and tumbling, tumultuous torrents
Of virtuous abhorrence,
When loud as the challenging trumpets of John at Le-
    panto
Rings the clarion, "I don't want to."
This is the day, the season,
Of wrongs without reason,
The day when the prunes and the cereal
Taste like building material,
When the spinach tastes only like spinach, and honey
    and sugar

Raise howls like the yowls of a quarrelsome puma or
    cougar,
When the wail is not to be hushed
Nor the hair to be brushed,
When life is frustration, and either
A person must be all alone or have somebody with her,
    and tolerates neither,
When outdoors is worse than in, and indoors than out,
    and both too dull to be borne,
And dolls are flung under the bed and books are torn,
When people humiliate a person
With their clumsily tactful attempts to conciliate a per-
    son,
When music no charm possesses,
Nor hats, nor mittens, nor dresses,
When the frowning fortress is woe
And the watchword is No.
You owners of children who pass this day with for-
    bearance,
You indeed are parents!

The City

HERE men walk alone
    For most of their lives,
What with hydrants for dogs,
And windows for wives.

Hearts of Gold
or
A Good Excuse Is Worse Than None

THERE are some people who are very resourceful
    At being remorseful,
And who apparently feel that the best way to make
    friends
Is to do something terrible and then make amends.
They come to your party and make a great hit with your
    Victorian aunt and with her freely mingle,
And suddenly after another drink they start a lot of
    double entendre the *entendre* of which is unfortu-
    nately not *double* but single,
And if you say anything to them they take umbrage,
And later when you are emptying the ash trays before
    going to bed you find them under the sofa where
    they have crept for a good night's slumbrage.
Then next day they are around intoning apologies
With all the grace and conviction of a high-paid choir
    intoning doxologies.
There are people in every group
Who will jog your elbow at table just when you are
    lifting a spoonful of very hot soup,
Or at a musicale or something while you're listening to
    a ravishing obbligato
Will forget their cigarettes and burn a hole in your
    clothes the size of a medium-sized tomato.

And then you are presented with a lot of form-fitting
    apologies
Quite good enough, I am sure, for inclusion in one of
    the higher-class anthologies.
Everybody says these people have hearts of gold,
But nevertheless they're always talking when you're put-
    ting, or splashing mud on you from their car, or
    giving you a cold,
And they are always sure that today you don't mind their
    inflicting on you any sorrow,
Because they'll give you so much pleasure when they
    smilingly apologize tomorrow,
But I myself would rather have a rude word from some-
    one who has done me no harm
Than a graceful letter from the King of England saying
    he's sorry he broke my arm.

It's a Grand Parade It Will Be,
Modern Design

Saint Patrick was a proper man, a man to be admired;
Of numbering his virtues I am never, never tired.
A handsome man, a holy man, a man of mighty deeds,
He walked the lanes of Erin, a-telling of his beads.
A-telling of his beads, he was, and spreading of the word.
I think that of Saint Patrick's Day, Saint Patrick hadn't
    heard.

The saint was born a subject of the ancient British
    throne,
But the Irish in their wisdom recognized him as their
    own.
A raiding party captured him, and carried him away,
And Patrick loved the Irish, and he lived to capture they,
A-walking of the valleys and a-spreading of the word.
I think that of Saint Patrick's Day, Saint Patrick hadn't
    heard.

He defied the mighty Druids, he spoke them bold and
    plain,
And he lit the Easter fire on the lofty hill of Shane.
He lit the Easter fire where the hill and heaven met,
And on every hill in Ireland the fire is burning yet.
He lit the Easter fire, a-spreading of the word.
I think that of Saint Patrick's Day, Saint Patrick hadn't
    heard.

Saint Patrick was a proper man before he was a saint,
He was shaky in his Latin, his orthography was quaint,
But he walked the length of Ireland, her mountains and
her lakes,
A-building of his churches and a-driving out the snakes,
A-building of his churches and a-spreading of the word.
I think that of Saint Patrick's Day, Saint Patrick hadn't
heard.

But the radio announcer is ever in the vogue;
He ushers in Saint Patrick with a rolling Broadway
brogue,
He oils the vernal air waves with macushlas and col-
leens,
Begorras, worra-worras, and spurious spalpeens.
If Saint Francis had a sponsor, we would hear him as a
thrush,
And Saint George would cackle cockney.
Saint Patrick, here's my blush.

Kindly Unhitch That Star, Buddy

I HARDLY suppose I know anybody who wouldn't rather
be a success than a failure,

Just as I suppose every piece of crabgrass in the garden
would much rather be an azalea,

And in celestial circles all the run-of-the-mill angels
would rather be archangels or at least cherubim
and seraphim,

And in the legal world all the little process-servers hope
to grow up into great big bailiffim and sheriffim.

Indeed, everybody wants to be a wow,

But not everybody knows exactly how.

Some people think they will eventually wear diamonds
instead of rhinestones

Only by everlastingly keeping their noses to their ghrine-
stones,

And other people think they will be able to put in more
time at Palm Beach and the Ritz

By not paying too much attention to attendance at the
office but rather in being brilliant by starts and fits.

Some people after a full day's work sit up all night getting a college education by correspondence,

While others seem to think they'll get just as far by de-
voting their evenings to the study of the difference
in temperament between brunettance and blond-
ance.

In short, the world is filled with people trying to achieve
success,

And half of them think they'll get it by saying No and
    half of them by saying Yes,

And if all the ones who say No said Yes, and vice versa,
    such is the fate of humanity that ninety-nine per
    cent of them still wouldn't be any better off than
    they were before,

Which perhaps is just as well because if everybody was
    a success nobody could be contemptuous of any-
    body else and everybody would start in all over
    again trying to be a bigger success than everybody
    else so they would have somebody to be contemptu-
    ous of and so on forevermore,

Because when people start hitching their wagons to a
    star,

That's the way they are.

Lament on the Eve of Parting

I SHALL grieve, I grieve, I am grieving.
  Abel is leaving.
Abel, the wise and the clever,
Is leaving, is leaving forever.
He goes to a wealthy tycoon
For an extra five dollars a moon,
Abel, the kind and gentle
Whose faults, if any, were minor and incidental.
North Carolina was his native heath
And the gold in his heart ran all the way up to his teeth.
Abel, the courtly and portly,
Is departing shortly.
Never were white shoes whitened or tan shoes tanned
As beneath his caressing hand,
Nor the silver and glass so luminous
As beneath those fingers bituminous.
Did a faucet leak, did the furnace refuse to function?
Abel had straightened it out between breakfast and
  luncheon.
Did a fuse blow, or a bulb flicker and die like the flame
  of plum-pudding brandy?
He had always a new one handy.
Did a guest request a harpoon, a harp, a tarpaulin, a
  tarpon, a turpentine hipbath, a hymnal, let the guest
  request what he would,
Abel would either produce, or rig up something as good.

He could string a radio aerial
Or lay out a person for burial.
His voice dark honey dripping from an olden golden
funnel
And his "Suh" was as good as a "Cunnel."
Farewell, Abel, good-by,
You recede from my misty eye,
You have left to join your tycoon
For five more dollars a moon.
O Abel, no longer visible,
Abel, I'm misible!

Glossina Morsitans, *or, the Tsetse*

A GLOSSINA MORSITANS bit rich Aunt Betsy.
   Tsk tsk, tsetse.

"My Child Is Phlegmatic . . ."
—Anxious Parent

ANXIOUS Parent, I guess you have just never been
  around;

I guess you just don't know who are the happiest people
    anywhere to be found;

So you are worried, are you, because your child is turn-
    ing out to be phlegmatic?

Forgive me if I seem a trifle unsympathatic.

Why do you want your child to be a flashing, coruscating
    gem?

Don't you know the only peace the world can give lies
    not in flame but in phlegm?

Don't you know that the people with souls of putty

Are the only people who are sitting prutty?

They never get all worked up at the drop of a pin or a
    feather or a hat,

They never go around saying bitterly to themselves:
    "Oh God, did I really do, did I really say *that*?"

They never boil over when they read about stool pigeons
    getting girls into reformatories by making treacher-
    ous advances;

They never get perfectly futilely harrowed about Sacco
and Vanzetti, or Alice Adamses who don't have good
times at dances;

They never blink an eyelash about colleges that are going
to the dogs because of football overemphasis;

They never almost die with indignation when some col-
ored person is lynched in Natchez or Memphis.

No, when they eat they digest their food, and when they
go to bed they get right to sleep,

And four phlegmatic angels a stolid watch over them
keep.

Oh to be phlegmatic, oh to be stolid, oh to be torpid, oh
to be calm!

For it is only thus, Anxious Parent, that we can get
through life without a qualm.

Birth Comes to the Archbishop

MINISTERS
    Don't like bar sinisters.
They consider that sort of irregularity
As the height of vulgarity
And go around making remarks
About the need for patrolling the beaches and parks.
They hate to see any deadlock
Between sin and wedlock
And get very nervous
When people omit the marriage service.
They regard as villains
Owners of unauthorized chillains,
A point of view
Which of course doesn't embarrass me or you
But makes things very inconvenient
For many really quite nice girls who may have been just
    a bit lenient.
So although none of us is in danger
Of the arrival of an inexplicable little stranger
Still I think we ought to join with a lot of others
And wish the best of luck to the nation's unmarried
    mothers.

Creeps and Crawls

THE insect world appealed to Fabre.
I find the insect world macabre.
In every hill of ants I see
A governed glimpse of what shall be,
And sense in every web contriver
Man's predecessor and survivor.
Someday, perhaps, my citronella
Will rank with Chamberlain's umbrella.

A Carol for Children

GOD rest you, merry Innocents,
  Let nothing you dismay,
Let nothing wound an eager heart
Upon this Christmas day.

Yours be the genial holly wreaths,
The stockings and the tree;
An aged world to you bequeaths
Its own forgotten glee.

Soon, soon enough come crueler gifts,
The anger and the tears;
Between you now there sparsely drifts
A handful yet of years.

Oh, dimly, dimly glows the star
Through the electric throng;
The bidding in temple and bazaar
Drowns out the silver song.

The ancient altars smoke afresh,
The ancient idols stir;
Faint in the reek of burning flesh
Sink frankincense and myrrh.

Gaspar, Balthazar, Melchior!
Where are your offerings now?

What greetings to the Prince of War,
His darkly branded brow?

Two ultimate laws alone we know,
The ledger and the sword—
So far away, so long ago,
We lost the infant Lord.

Only the children clasp his hand;
His voice speaks low to them,
And still for them the shining band
Wings over Bethlehem.

God rest you, merry Innocents,
While innocence endures.
A sweeter Christmas than we to ours
May you bequeath to yours.

Homeward Bund

BE CAREFUL not to hate the moth,
　　It isn't she who eats your cloth,
But only little ones of hers
That lunch on tweeds and dine on furs.
Who but a jingo his heart could steel
To spray these innocents out of a meal?
My heart is mush, so come on, larvæ,
My closet's full, and I'm Fred Harvey.

One Night in Oz

O SHE whom I cannot abide,
  Our hostess sat us side by side,
But must the heavy silence scream
Our heartfelt mutual disesteem?
Can we not mitigate our plight
If you turn left and I turn right?
This tasty fare will tastier taste
If by each other we are not faced;
Why shouldn't our acquaintance end,
Friend of a friend of a friend of a friend?
You do not love my way of life,
Myself, my children or my wife,
And too self-satisfied for tact,
Don't bother to conceal the fact,
While I my feelings may not hint
Till I can set them forth in print.
Our juxtaposition as we dine
Results from no intrigue of mine.
You'd wished yon titled refugee
Whose dollars Clippered here with he,
While I, whose hopes are mild and mere,
Had but desired to not be here.
Discovering who sits next to who,
Your face fell one inch, mine fell two.
Yet o'er our hostess's well-meant food
Did I refrain from being rude,
A minor courtesy which I grieve

To note that you could not achieve.
Well, Madam, if you wish it so,
Hitch up your girdle, here we go.
O living sneer, poor painted peril,
Yours is the snobbery of the sterile.
Three husbands have you unbeguiled,
And here you stand without a child.
Of hounds and huntin' you discourse
Who never sat upon a horse.
You, who have never penned a line
That would not shame a Bantu of nine,
Serve up the great as chummy nicknames
And little intimate make-you-sick names.
How glibly in your talk you glue
Bohemia to Park Avenue,
Unwitting that your gossipy speech
Stamps you a hanger-on in each.
Ah, let us our acquaintance end,
Friend of Hemingway's friend's friend's friend;
I'm just as glad as glad can be
To feel towards you as you towards me.

Midsummer Warning

AUGUST is sunburn and moonlight,
    August's a menace to men;
When the casual canoer discovers l'amouer,
August has done it again.
August is moonlight and sunburn,
When the bachelor sows as he reaps;
His sunburn will finally unburn,
But he's burned in the moonlight for keeps

Anatomical Reflection

SALLY RAND
    Needs an extra hand.

To My Valentine

MORE than a catbird hates a cat,
  Or a criminal hates a clue,
Or the Axis hates the United States,
That's how much I love you.

I love you more than a duck can swim,
And more than a grapefruit squirts,
I love you more than gin rummy is a bore,
And more than a toothache hurts.

As a shipwrecked sailor hates the sea,
Or a juggler hates a shove,
As a hostess detests unexpected guests,
That's how much you I love.

I love you more than a wasp can sting,
And more than the subway jerks,
I love you as much as a beggar needs a crutch,
And more than a hangnail irks.

I swear to you by the stars above,
And below, if such there be,
As the High Court loathes perjurious oaths,
That's how you're loved by me.

The Smelt

OH, WHY does man pursue the smelt?
It has no valuable pelt,
It boasts of no escutcheon royal,
It yields no ivory or oil,
Its life is dull, its death is tame,
A fish as humble as its name.
Yet—take this salmon somewhere else.
And bring me half a dozen smelts.

Celery

CELERY, raw,
 Develops the jaw,
But celery, stewed,
Is more quietly chewed.

The Cantaloupe

ONE cantaloupe is ripe and lush,
 Another's green, another's mush.
I'd buy a lot more cantaloupe
If I possessed a fluoroscope.

The Eel

I DON'T mind eels
 Except as meals.

England Expects

Let us pause to consider the English,
  Who when they pause to consider themselves they
    get all reticently thrilled and tinglish,
Because every Englishman is convinced of one thing,
    viz.:
That to be an Englishman is to belong to the most ex-
    clusive club there is:
A club to which benighted bounders of Frenchmen and
    Germans and Italians et cetera cannot even aspire
    to belong,
Because they don't even speak English, and the Ameri-
    cans are worst of all because they speak it wrong.
Englishmen are distinguished by their traditions and
    ceremonials,
And also by their affection for their colonies and their
    contempt for their colonials.
When foreigners ponder world affairs, why sometimes
    by doubts they are smitten,
But Englishmen know instinctively that what the world
    needs most is whatever is best for Great Britain.
They have a splendid navy and they conscientiously
    admire it,
And every English schoolboy knows that John Paul
    Jones was only an unfair American pirate.
English people disclaim sparkle and verve,
But speak without reservations of their Anglo-Saxon re-
    serve.

After listening to little groups of English ladies and
gentlemen at cocktail parties and in hotels and
Pullmans, of defining Anglo-Saxon reserve I despair,
But I think it consists of assuming that nobody else is
there,
And I shudder to think where Anglo-Saxon reserve ends
when I consider where it begins,
Which is in a few high-pitched statements of what one's
income is and just what foods give one a rash and
whether one and one's husband or wife sleep in a
double bed or twins.
All good young Englishmen go to Oxford or Cambridge
and they all write and publish books before their
graduation,
And I often wondered how they did it until I realized
that they have to do it because their genteel accents
are so developed that they can no longer understand each other's spoken words so the written word
is their only means of intercommunication.
England is the last home of the aristocracy, and the art
of protecting the aristocracy from the encroach-
ments of commerce has been raised to quite an art,
Because in America a rich butter-and-egg man is only a
rich butter-and-egg man or at most an honorary
LL.D. of some hungry university, but in England
why before he knows it he is Sir Benjamin Buttery,
Bart.
Anyhow, I think the English people are sweet.

And we might as well get used to them because when they slip and fall they always land on their own or somebody else's feet.

Waiting for the Birdie

Some hate broccoli, some hate bacon,
        I hate having my picture taken.
How can your family claim to love you
And then demand a picture of you?
The electric chair is a comfortable chair,
But I know an equally comfortless pair;
One is the dentist's, my good sirs,
And the other is the photographer's.
Oh, the fly in all domestic ointments
Is affectionate people who make appointments
To have your teeth filled left and right,
Or your face reproduced in black and white.
You open the door and you enter the studio,
And you feel less cheerio than nudio.
The hard light shines like seventy suns,
And you know that your features are foolish ones.
The photographer says, Natural, please,
And you cross your knees and uncross your knees.
Like a duke in a high society chronicle
The camera glares at you through its monocle
And you feel ashamed of your best attire,
Your nose itches, your palms perspire,
Your muscles stiffen, and all the while
You smile and smile and smile and smile.
It's over; you weakly grope for the door;
It's not; the photographer wants one more.
And if this experience you survive,

Wait, just wait till the proofs arrive.
You look like a drawing by Thurber or Bab,
Or a gangster stretched on a marble slab.
And all your dear ones, including your wife,
Say There he is, that's him to the life!
Some hate broccoli, some hate bacon,
But I hate having my picture taken.

Shrinking Song

Woollen socks, woollen socks!
Full of color, full of clocks!
Plain and fancy, yellow, blue,
From the counter beam at you.
O golden fleece, O magic flocks!
O irresistible woollen socks!
O happy haberdasher's clerk
Amid that galaxy to work!
And now it festers, now it rankles
Not to have them round your ankles;
Now with your conscience do you spar;
They look expensive, and they are;
Now conscience whispers, You ought not to,
And human nature roars, You've got to!
Woollen socks, woollen socks!
First you buy them in a box.
You buy them several sizes large,
Fit for Hercules, or a barge.
You buy them thus because you think
These lovely woollen socks may shrink.
At home you don your socks with ease,
You find the heels contain your knees;
You realize with saddened heart
Their toes and yours are far apart.
You take them off and mutter Bosh,
You up and send them to the wash.
Too soon, too soon the socks return,

Too soon the horrid truth you learn;
Your woollen socks can not be worn
Unless a midget child is born,
And either sockless you must go,
Or buy a sock for every toe.
Woollen socks, woollen socks!
Infuriating paradox!
Hosiery wonderful and terrible,
Heaven to wear, and yet unwearable.
The man enmeshed in such a quandary
Can only hie him to the laundry,
And while his socks are hung to dry,
Wear them once as they're shrinking by.

Absence Makes the Heart Grow
Heart Trouble

I KNOW a girl who is in Paris, France,
   And I fear that every evening she goes out to dance,
And she ought to be pining for the undersigned,
But I fear that nothing is further from her mind,
And what is very suspicious, her letters say that she
   is being very quiet,
But my nerves deny it,
And I am unhappily sure that she is drinking champagne
   with aristocrats,
And exchanging cynicisms with sophistocrats.
She goes walking in the *Bois*
With elegant young men who are not *moi*.
She is receiving compliments from ambassadors,
And riding in fiacres with foreign agents who cry that
   for her they would betray the secrets of their lords
   and massadors.
Artists to have her pose for them are clamoring,
Tenors and symphony conductors tempt her with their
   entire repertoire from Pagliacci to Götterdämmer-
   ung;
Argentines and Brazilians
Seek to dazzle her with their dazzling millions;
Men of the world with etchings and monocles
Plead with her to become part of their personal chron-
   icles;

Aides and equerries try to explain without too much
    bluntness and yet without too much shyness
The advantages a girl or a tailor enjoys when he or she
    is entitled to the subtitle of By Appointment to
    His Royal Highness.
Trips abroad are very nice for Davis Cup teams and
    Olympic teams, and that's about all you can say for
    them,
Because I think that when you are fond of somebody
    you would rather be with them than away from
    them,
So I wish that time would suddenly advance,
Because I want to be standing on the dock trying to
    find somebody on deck who will undoubtedly be
    wearing a terribly smart and perfectly terrible hat
    which she bought in Paris, France.

I'll Get One Tomorrow

B ARBER, barber, come and get me;
     Hairy torrents irk and fret me.
Hair and hair again appears,
And climbs like ivy round my ears;
Hair across my collar gambols;
Down my neck it wayward ambles;
Ever down it trips and trickles,
Yes, and where it trips, it tickles.
Barber dear, I wish I knew
Why I do not visit you,
Why I grudge the minutes ten
In your sanitary den,
Why I choose to choke on hair
Rather than to mount your chair.
Men no busier than I
Weekly to your office hie;
Men no braver than myself
Confront the armory on your shelf;
Men no wealthier than me
Gladly meet your modest fee,
And for a fraction of a dollar
Keep the jungle off their collar.
I alone am shy and flustered,
A solitary, cowardly custard,
Shaggy as a prize Angora,
Overrun with creeping flora.
Barber, barber, you're in luck;

The bell has rung, the hour has struck.
Sloth is strong, but hair is stronger;
I cannot stand it any longer.
Barber, barber, here I come;
Shake up the odorous bay rum;
Bring on your shears, your scythes, your snippers,
Bring on your crisp, electric clippers;
Employ a dozen extra sweepers;
Bring giant harvesters and reapers;
I warn you that a bumper crop
Waits to overwhelm your shop.
Barber, barber, be verbose,
Be anything, but clip me close;
Leave me razored, leave me scissored.
Leave me hairless as a lizard;
Barber, barber, singe and scald;
Barber, can't you make me bald?
I'd be the happiest of men,
And never think of you again.

Washington's Birthday Eve

GEORGE WASHINGTON was a gentleman,
    A soldier and a scholar;
He crossed the Delaware with a boat,
The Potomac, with a dollar.
The British faced him full of joy,
And departed full of sorrow;
George Washington was a gentleman.
His birthday is tomorrow.

When approached by fellow patriots,
And asked for his opinion,
He spoke in accents clear and bold,
And, probably, Virginian.
His winter home at Valley Forge
Was underheated, rather.
He possessed a sturdy Roman nose,
And became his country's father.

His army was a hungry horde,
Ill-armed, worse-clad Colonials;
He was our leading President,
And discouraged ceremonials.
His portrait on our postage stamps,
It does him less than justice;
He was much respected by his wife,
The former Mrs. Custis.

He routed George's scarlet coats;
(Though oft by Congress hindered)
When they fortified the leeward side,
He slashed them from the windward.
He built and launched our Ship of State,
He brought it safe to harbor;
He wore no beard upon his chin,
Thanks to his faithful barber.

George Washington was a gentleman,
His birthday is tomorrow.
He filled his country's friends with joy,
His country's foes, with sorrow.
And so my dears, his grateful land
In robes of glory clad him.
George Washington was a gentleman.
I'm glad his parents had him.

The Anatomy of Happiness

Lots of truisms don't have to be repeated but there is
one that has got to be,

Which is that it is much nicer to be happy than it is
not to be,

And I shall even add to it by stating unequivocally and
without restraint

That you are much happier when you are happy than
when you ain't.

Some people are just naturally Pollyanna,

While others call for sugar and cream and strawberries
on their manna.

Now, I think we all ought to say a fig for the happiness
that comes of thinking helpful thoughts and search-
ing your soul,

The most exciting happiness is the happiness generated
by forces beyond your control,

Because if you just depend on your helpful thoughts
for your happiness and would just as soon drink
buttermilk as champagne, and if mink is no better
than lapin to you,

Why you don't even deserve to have anything nice and
exciting happen to you.

If you are really Master of your Fate,

It shouldn't make any difference to you whether Cleopatra or the Bearded Lady is your mate,

So I hold no brief for the kind of happiness or the kind

of unhappiness that some people constantly carry around in their breast,

Because that kind of happiness simply consists of being resigned to the worst just as that kind of unhappiness consists of being resentful of the best.

No, there is only one kind of happiness that I take the stump for,

Which is the kind that comes when something so wonderful falls in your lap that joy is what you jump for,

Something not of your own doing,

When the blue sky opens and out pops a refund from the Government or an invitation to a terrapin dinner or an unhoped for yes from the lovely creature you have been disconsolately wooing.

And obviously such miracles don't happen every day,

But here's hoping they may,

Because then everybody would be happy except the people who pride themselves on creating their own happiness who as soon as they saw everybody who didn't create their own happiness happy they would probably grieve over sharing their own heretofore private sublimity,

A condition which I could face with equanimity.

No Wonder Our Fathers Died

Does anybody mind if I don't live in a house that is quaint?

Because, for one thing, quaint houses are generally houses where plumbing ain't,

And while I don't hold with fanatical steel-and-glass modernistic bigots,

Still, I do think that it simplifies life if you live it surrounded by efficient pipes and faucets and spiggots.

I admit that wells and pumps and old oaken buckets are very nice in a poem or ode,

But I feel that in literature is where they should have their permanent abode,

Because suppose you want a bath,

It is pleasanter to be able to take it without leaving a comfortable stuffy room and going out into the bracing fresh air and bringing back some water from the end of a path.

Another thing about which I am very earnest,

Is that I do like a house to be properly furnaced,

Because if I am out in the bracing fresh air I expect to be frozen,

But to be frigid in a stuffy room isn't what I would have chosen.

And when you go to bed in a quaint house the whole house grumbles and mutters,

And you are sure the walls will be shattered by clatter-
ing shutters.

At least you hope it's the shutters but you fear it's a
gang of quaint ghosts warming up for twelve o'clock,

And you would lock yourself snugly in but the quaint
old key won't turn in the quaint old lock,

So you would pull the bedclothes snugly up over your
head and lie there till a year from next autumn,

Were it not a peculiarity of bedclothes in quaint houses
that if you pull them up on top, why your feet stick
out at the bautum,

But anyhow you find a valley among the hilltops of
your mattress and after a while slumber comes
softly stealing,

And that is when you feel a kiss on your cheek and you
think maybe it is a goodnight kiss from your guard-
ian angel, but it isn't, it's a leak in the ceiling.

Oh, I yield to none in my admiration of the hardy
colonist and their hardy spouses,

But I still feel that their decadent descendants build
more comfortable houses.

The Hippopotamus

BEHOLD the hippopotamus!
   We laugh at how he looks to us,
And yet in moments dank and grim
I wonder how we look to him.
Peace, peace, thou hippopotamus!
We really look all right to us,
As you no doubt delight the eye
Of other hippopotami.

Where There's a Will, There's Velleity

SEATED one day at the dictionary I was pretty weary
and also pretty ill at ease,
Because a word I had always liked turned out not to
be a word at all, and suddenly I found myself
among the v's,
And suddenly among the v's I came across a new word
which was a word called *velleity*,
So the new word I found was better than the old word
I lost, for which I thank my tutelary deity,
Because velleity is a word which gives me great satis-
faction,
Because do you know what it means, it means *low degree
of volition not prompting to action*,
And I always knew I had something holding me back
but I didn't know what,
And it's quite a relief to know it isn't a conspiracy, it's
only velleity that I've got,
Because to be wonderful at everything has always been
my ambition,
Yes indeed, I am simply teeming with volition,
So why I never was wonderful at anything was some-
thing I couldn't see
While all the time, of course, my volition was merely
volition of a low degree,
Which is the kind of volition that you are better off with-
out it,

Because it puts an idea in your head but doesn't prompt
   you to do anything about it.
So you think it would be nice to be a great pianist but
   why bother with practising for hours at the key-
   board,
Or you would like to be the romantic captain of a romantic ship but can't find time to study navigation
   or charts of the ocean or the seaboard;
You want a lot of money but you are not prepared to
   work for it,
Or a book to read in bed but you do not care to go into
   the nocturnal cold and murk for it;
And now if you have any such symptoms you can identify
   your malady with accurate spontaneity:
It's velleity,
So don't forget to remember that you're velleitous, and
   if anybody says you're just lazy,
Why, they're crazy.

Kind of an Ode to Duty

O Duty,
    Why hast thou not the visage of a sweetie or a
    cutie?
Why displayest thou the countenance of the kind of con-
    scientious organizing spinster
That the minute you see her you are aginster?
Why glitter thy spectacles so ominously?
Why art thou clad so abominously?
Why art thou so different from Venus
And why do thou and I have so few interests mutually
    in common between us?
Why art thou fifty per cent. martyr
And fifty-one per cent. Tartar?
Why is it thy unfortunate wont
To try to attract people by calling on them either to
    leave undone the deeds they like, or to do the deeds
    they don't?
Why art thou so like an April post mortem
Or something that died in the ortumn?
Above all, why dost thou continue to hound me?
Why art thou always albatrossly hanging around me?
Thou so ubiquitous,
And I so iniquitous.
I seem to be the one person in the world thou art per-
    petually preaching at who or to who;
Whatever looks like fun, there art thou standing between
    me and it, calling yoo-hoo.

O Duty, Duty!

How noble a man should I be hadst thou the visage of a
sweetie or a cutie!

Wert thou but houri instead of hag

Then would my halo indeed be in the bag!

But as it is thou art so much forbiddinger than a Wode-
house hero's forbiddingest aunt

That in the words of the poet, When Duty whispers low,
Thou must, this erstwhile youth replies, I just can't.

Prayer at the End of a Rope

Dear Lord, observe this bended knee,
This visage meek and humble,
And heed this confidential plea,
Voiced in a reverent mumble.

I ask no miracles nor stunts,
No heavenly radiogram;
I only beg for once, just once,
To not be in a jam.

One little moment thy servant craves
Of being his own master;
One placid vale between the waves
Of duty and disaster.

Oh, when the postman's whistle shrills,
Just once, Lord, let me grin:
Let me have settled last month's bills
Before this month's come in.

Let me not bite more off the cob
Than I have teeth to chew;
Please let me finish just one job
Before the next is due.

Consider, too, my social life,
Sporadic though it be;

Why is it only mental strife
That pleasure brings to me?

For months, when people entertain,
Me they do not invite;
Then suddenly invitations rain,
All for the self-same night.

R.S.V.P.'s I pray thee send
Alone and not in bunches,
Or teach me I cannot attend
Two dinners or two lunches.

Let me my hostess not insult,
Not call her diamonds topaz;
Else harden me to the result
Of my fantastic faux pas.

One little lull, Lord, that's my plea,
Then loose the storm again;
Just once, this once, I beg to be
Not in a jam. Amen.

A Brief Guide to New York

IN NEW YORK beautiful girls can become more beauti-
    ful by going to Elizabeth Arden
And getting stuff put on their faces and waiting for it to
    harden,
And poor girls with nothing to their names but a letter
    or two can get rich and joyous
From a brief trip to their loyous.
So I can say with impunity
That New York is a city of opportunity.
It also has many fine theaters and hotels,
And a lot of taxis, buses, subways and els,
Best of all, if you don't show up at the office or at a tea
    nobody will bother their head
They will just think you are dead.
That's why I really think New York is exquisite.
And some day I'm going to pay it a visit.

Incompetent and Immaterial

THERE was a lady loved a gent,
   But her reward was meager.
Said her gentleman friend to his gentleman friends,
The lady's overeager.

There was a lady loved a gent,
She held her backbone rigid.
Said her gentleman friend to his gentleman friends,
The lady's far too frigid.

There was a lady loved herself,
But equipped with Cold and Hot.
Said her gentleman friends to their gentleman friends,
Whatever it is, she's got.

Oh let us laugh at the lines above,
Less precious than pearls and rubies—
Telling the ladies what ladies know,
That gentlemen *all* are boobies.

Biological Reflection

A GIRL whose cheeks are covered with paint
   Has an advantage with me over one whose ain't.

The Mind of Professor Primrose

MY STORY begins in the town of Cambridge, Mass.,
    Home of the Harvard Business and Dental
    Schools,
And more or less the home of Harvard College.
Now, Harvard is a cultural institution,
Squandering many a dollar upon professors,
As a glance at a Harvard football team makes obvious;
Professors wise and prowling in search of wisdom,
And every mother's son of them absent-minded.
But the absentest mind belonged to Professor Primrose.
He had won a Nobel award and a Pulitzer Prize,
A Guggenheim and a leg on the Davis Cup,
But he couldn't remember to shave both sides of his face.
He discharged the dog and took the cook for an airing;
He frequently lit his hair and combed his cigar;
He set a trap for the baby and dandled the mice;
He wound up his key and opened the door with his
    watch;
He tipped his students and flunked the traffic police-
    man;
He fed the mosquitoes crumbs and slapped at the
    robins;
He always said his prayers when he entered the theater
And left the church for a smoke between the acts;
He mixed the exterminator man a cocktail
And told his guests to go way, he had no bugs;
He rode the streets on a bicycle built for two,

And he never discovered he wasn't teaching at Yale.
At last one summer he kissed his crimson flannels
And packed his wife in camphor, and she complained.
She had always hated camphor, and she complained.
"My dear," she ordered, "these *contretemps* must cease;
You must bring this absent mind a little bit nearer;
You must tidy up that disorderly cerebellum;
You must write today and enroll in the Pelman Institute."
He embraced his pen and took his wife in hand,
He wrinkled a stamp and thoughtfully licked his brow,
He wrote the letter and mailed it, and what do you know?
In a couple of days he disappeared from Cambridge.
"For heaven's sake, my husband has disappeared,"
Said Mrs. Primrose. "Now isn't that just like him?"
And she cut the meat and grocery orders in half,
And moved the chairs in the living room around,
And settled down to a little solid comfort.
She had a marvelous time for seven years,
At the end of which she took a train to Chicago.
She liked to go to Chicago once in a while
Because of a sister-in-law who lived in Cambridge.
Her eye was caught at Schenectady by the porter;
She noticed that he was brushing off a dime,
And trying to put the passenger in his pocket.
"Porter," she said, "aren't you Professor Primrose?
Aren't you my husband, the missing Professor Primrose?

And what did you learn at the Pelman Institute?"
"Mah Lawd, Maria," the porter said, "mah Lawd!
Did you say *Pelman*? Ah wrote to de *Pullman* folks!

I Never Even Suggested It

I KNOW lots of men who are in love and lots of men
  who are married and lots of men who are both,
And to fall out with their loved ones is what all of them
  are most loth.
They are conciliatory at every opportunity,
Because all they want is serenity and a certain amount
  of impunity.
Yes, many the swain who has finally admitted that the
  earth is flat
Simply to sidestep a spat,
Many the masculine Positively or Absolutely which has
  been diluted to an If
Simply to avert a tiff,
Many the two-fisted executive whose domestic conver-
  sation is limited to a tactfully interpolated Yes,
And then he is amazed to find that he is being raked
  backwards over a bed of coals nevertheless.
These misguided fellows are under the impression that
  it takes two to make a quarrel, that you can side-
  step a crisis by nonaggression and nonresistance,
Instead of removing yourself to a discreet distance.
Passivity can be a provoking *modus operandi*;
Consider the Empire and Gandhi.
Silence is golden, but sometimes invisibility is golder.
Because loved ones may not be able to make bricks with-
  out straw but often they don't need any straw to

manufacture a bone to pick or blood in their eye or
   a chip for their soft white shoulder.
It is my duty, gentlemen, to inform you that women are
   dictators all, and I recommend to you this moral:
In real life it takes only one to make a quarrel.

My Dear, How Ever Did You Think Up
This Delicious Salad?

THIS is a very sad ballad,
   Because it's about the way too many people make
   a salad.
Generally they start with bananas,
And they might just as well use gila monsters or iguanas.
Pineapples are another popular ingredient,
Although there is one school that holds preserved pears
   or peaches more expedient,
And you occasionally meet your fate
In the form of a prune or a date.
Rarely you may chance to discover a soggy piece of
   tomato looking very forlorn and Cinderella-ry,
But for the most part you are confronted by apples and
   celery,
And it's not a bit of use at this point to turn pale or
   break out in a cold perspiration,
Because all this is only the foundation,
Because if you think the foundation sounds unenticing,
Just wait until we get to the dressing, or rather, the icing.
There are various methods of covering up the body, and
   to some, marshmallows are the pall supreme,
And others prefer whipped cream,
And then they deck the grave with ground-up peanuts
   and maraschinos
And you get the effect of a funeral like Valentino's,

And about the only thing that in this kind of salad is
    never seen
Is any kind of green,
And oil and vinegar and salt and pepper are at a mini-
    mum,
But there is a maximum of sugar and syrup and ginger
    and nutmeg and cinnamum,
And my thoughts about this kind of salad are just as
    unutterable
As parsnips are unbutterable,
And indeed I am surprised that the perpetrators haven't
    got around to putting buttered parsnips in these sal-
    magundis,
And the salad course nowadays seems to be a month of
    sundaes.

What's the Use?

SURE, deck your lower limbs in pants;
    Yours are the limbs, my sweeting.
You look divine as you advance—
Have you seen yourself retreating?

The Party Next Door

I TRUST I am not a spoil sport, but there is one thing I
deplore,
And that is a party next door,
If there is anything that gives me tantrums galore
It is a party next door.
I do not know how we came into this world, or what for,
But it was not, I am sure, to listen to a party next door.
I am by nature very fond of everybody, even my neigh-
bors,
And I think it only right that they should enjoy some
kind of diversion after their labors,
But why don't they get their diversion by going to the
movies or the Little Theater or the Comédie Fran-
çaise or the Commedia dell'arte?
Why do they always have to be giving a party?
You may think you have heard a noise because you have
heard an artillery barrage or an avalanche or the
subway's horrendous roar,
But you have never really heard anything until you have
heard a party next door.
You may have survived the impact of a gangster's bullet
or a hit-and-run driver or a bolt of lightning or the
hammer of Thor,
But you really don't know what an impact is until you
have felt the impact of a party next door.
A party next door never really gets going until you are
trying for some much-needed sleep,

And when it does get going, why awake is much easier
than your temper to keep.
At a party next door the guests stampede like elephants
in wooden shoes and gallop like desperate polo
players,
And all the women are coloratura sopranos and all the
men are train announcers and hog callers and saxo-
phone solo players.
They all have screamingly funny stories to tell to each
other,
And half of them get at one end of the house and half of
them get at the other end of the yard and then they
yell to each other.
The spirit is one of lawlessness and mockery,
And its audible symbols are giggles and squeals and guf-
faws and splintering furniture and crashing crock-
ery.
And even if the patrolman looks in from his beat they
do not moderate or stop,
No, they just seduce the cop.
And at last you manage to doze off by the dawn's early
light,
And they wake you up all over again shouting good
night,
And the host roars out to people to come back in for
a final cup,
And the windows rattle with horns blowing for wives
who can't find their bags, and engines being warmed
up,

And whether it consists of two quiet old ladies dropping
       in for a game of bridge or a lot of revelers getting
       really sort of out-of-bounds-like,
That's what a party next door always sounds like,
So when you see somebody with a hoarse voice and a
       pallid face and eyes bleary and red-rimmed and
       sore,
It doesn't mean they've been on a party themselves, no,
       it probably means that they have experienced a
       party next door.

The Japanese

How courteous is the Japanese;
 He always says, "Excuse it, please."
He climbs into his neighbor's garden,
And smiles, and says, "I beg your pardon";
He bows and grins a friendly grin,
And calls his hungry family in;
He grins, and bows a friendly bow;
"So sorry, this my garden now."

Traveler's Rest

I KNOW a renegade hotel.
  I also know I hate it well.
An inn so vile, an inn so shameless,
For very disgust I leave it nameless,
Loathing the name I will not utter,
Whose flavor reeks of rancid butter.
Five stories tall this mantrap stands,
With steps outstretched like welcoming hands,
And travelers, weary of their mileage,
Respond to its bright electric smileage.
They park their cars, and praise the Lord
For downy bed and toothsome board.
They pass unwary through its portals,
And every imp in Hades chortles.
Behold the regulars in the lobby;
Expectoration is their hobby.
Behold the loftiest of clerks:
He's manicuring as he works,
And bridles into dapper wrath
At a mild request for a room and bath.
Behold the niftiest of collars
Which murmurs, "That will be six dollars,"
The leer with innuendo rife.
Which says your wife is not your wife.
The doddering, halting elevator,
A contemporary of Poe or Pater.
The impudent boy with step that lags

Who snatches your coins and hides your bags;
The ill-fitting door to the musty room
That smells like a fairly empty tomb;
The bath you crave, being cramped and dusty
And the hot that turns out to be cold and rusty,
The towels clammy, the basin black,
And the bed that sags like a postman's back.
The dinner (two dollars and a quarter)
For the porterhouse that tastes like a porter.
The sleepy ascent to the room once more,
And the drunken Lothario next door,
Alone, and not wishing to be alone
Who roars his loves to the telephone.
You see that the beds are not turned down,
And you know the bedclothes are dank and brown,
And there isn't a thing to hang your clothes on,
And the sheet you shudder to place your toes on.
You search in vain for a bedside lamp,
You lose your slippers, the rug is damp,
The bulb in the ceiling is all in all,
And the switch is set in the furtherest wall.
A century later the night is past,
And you stagger down to break your fast.
Octoroon coffee, and shiny eggs
Semi-equipped with beaks and legs.
And you reach the desk and surrender your keys,
And the clerk sneers "Thirteen dollars, please,
Seven for meals and six for the room,
Do you know to who you are speaking to whom?

You can fry in Hell so long as you pay;
Stop in again when you pass our way!"
I know a renegade hotel.
1 also know I hate it well.
I'd name its name with my hand on the Bible,
But for disgust. And the laws of libel.

Riding on a Railroad Train

SOME people like to hitch and hike;
   They are fond of highway travel;
Their nostrils toil through gas and oil,
They choke on dust and gravel.
Unless they stop for the traffic cop
Their road is a fine-or-jail road,
But wise old I go rocketing by;
I'm riding on the railroad.

I love to loll like a limp rag doll
In a peripatetic *salon*;
To think and think of a long cool drink
And cry to the porter, *allons!*
Now the clickety clack of wheel on track
Grows clickety clackety clicker:
The line is clear for the engineer
And it mounts to his head like liquor.

Oh give me steel from roof to wheel,
But a soft settee to sit on,
And a cavalcade of commerce and trade
And a drummer to turn the wit on.
Stuyvesant chats with Kelly and Katz,
The professor warms to the broker,
And life is good in the brotherhood
Of an air-conditioned smoker.

With a farewell scream of escaping steam
The boiler bows to the Diesel;
The Iron Horse has run its course
And we ride a chromium weasel;
We draw our power from the harnessed shower,
The lightning without the thunder,
But a train is a train and will so remain
While the rails glide glistening under.

Oh, some like trips in luxury ships,
And some in gasoline wagons,
And others swear by the upper air
And the wings of flying dragons.
Let each make haste to indulge his taste,
Be it beer, champagne or cider;
My private joy, both man and boy,
Is being a railroad rider.

The Canary

THE song of canaries
    Never varies,
And when they're moulting
They're pretty revolting.

The Evening Out

You have your hat and coat on and she says she will
    be right down,

And you hope so because it is getting late and you are
    dining on the other side of town,

And you are pretty sure she can't take long,

Because when you left her she already looked as neat and
    snappy as a Cole Porter song,

So you stand around thinking of various things and won-
    dering why good rye costs more than Scotch,

And after a while you begin to look at your watch,

And so goes ten minutes, and then fifteen minutes, and
    then half an hour,

And you listen for the sound of water running because
    you suspect she may have gone back for a bath or
    a shower,

Or maybe she is taking a nap,

Or possibly getting up a subscription for the benefit of
    the children of the mouse that she said mean things
    about last night but she is now sorry got caught in
    a trap,

Or maybe she decided her hair was a mess and is now
    shampooing it,

But whatever she is up to, she is a long time doing it,

And finally she comes down and says she is sorry she
    couldn't find the right lipstick, that's why she was
    so slow,

And you look at her and she looks marvelous but not

a bit more marvelous than she did when you left
her forty-five minutes ago,

And you tell her she looks ravishing and she says No,
she is a sight,

And you reflect that you are now an hour late, but at
any rate she is now groomed for the rest of the
night,

So you get to your destination and there's the ladies'
dressing room and before you know it she's in it,

But she says she'll be back in a minute,

And so she is, but not to tarry,

No, only to ask you for her bag, which she has forgotten
she had asked you to carry,

So you linger in the lobby

And wish you had a nice portable hobby,

And you try to pass the time seeing how much you can
remember of the poetry you learned in school, both
good verse and bad verse,

And eventually she re-appears just about as you have decided she was in the middle of *Anthony Adverse,*

And she doesn't apologize, but glances at you as if you
were Bluebeard or Scrooge,

And says why didn't you tell her she had on too much
rouge?

And you look to see what new tint she has acquired,

And she looks just the same as she did before she retired,

So you dine, and reach the theater in time for the third
act, and then go somewhere to dance and sup,

And she says she looks like a scarecrow, she has to go
  straighten up,
So then you don't see her for quite a long time,
But at last you see her for a moment when she comes
  out to ask if you will lend her a dime,
The moral of all which is that you will have just as much
  of her company and still save considerable on cover
  charges and beverages and grub
If instead of taking her out on the town, you settle her in
  a nice comfortable dressing room and then go off
  and spend the evening at the Club.

The Politician

BEHOLD the politician.
  Self-preservation is his ambition.
He thrives in the D. of C.,
Where he was sent by you and me.

Whether elected or appointed
He considers himself the Lord's anointed,
And indeed the ointment lingers on him
So thick you can't get your fingers on him.

He has developed a sixth sense
About living at the public expense,
Because in private competition
He would encounter malnutrition.

He has many profitable hobbies
Not the least of which is lobbies.
He would not sell his grandmother for a quarter
If he suspected the presence of a reporter.

He gains votes ever and anew
By taking money from everybody and giving it to a few
While explaining that every penny
Was extracted from the few to be given to the many.

Some politicians are Republican, some Democratic,
And their feud is dramatic,

But except for the name
They are identically the same.

When a politician talks the foolishest,
And obstructs everything the mulishest,
And bellows the loudest,
Why his constituents are the proudest.

Wherever decent intelligent people get together
They talk about politicians as about bad weather,
But they are always too decent to go into politics them-
    selves and too intelligent even to go to the polls,
So I hope the kind of politicians they get will have no
    mercy on their pocketbooks or souls.

Read This Vibrant Exposé

Now curfew tolls in the old church steeple,
Bidding good night to sensible people;
Now thousands and thousands of people sensible
Think staying up later is reprehensible:
Now wives relentlessly bridge games terminate,
As thoughts of the morrow begin to germinate;
Now gangsters with pistols full of notches
Yawn discreetly and glance at their watches;
Now owls desist from to-wit-to-wooing,
And ne'er-do-wells from their ne'er-well-doing;
Now husband and wife and spouse and spouse
Unleash their cat and lock up their house;
Now celibates, of whom there are lots,
Wearily seek their lonely cots;
Now, in a word, the day is ended,
And a little sleep would be simply splendid.
But sleep is perverse as human nature,
Sleep is perverse as a legislature,
And holds that people who wish to sleep
Are people from whom away to keep.
Sleep, I am more than sorry to say,
Is deliberately half a world away.

The curfew that tolls in yonder steeple
Is unheard by a hemisphere of people.
Across the world, the alarm clock's reveille
Wakes foreigners drowsy and dishevelly;

Across the world the sun is aloft,
And people must rise from their mattresses soft,
And polish their teeth and shine their faces
And go to work in various places.
Now opens wide their portal of day,
And sleep, you might think, would go away,
Sleep would abandon that hemisphere
And distribute its favors over here.
But sleep is perverse as human nature,
Sleep is perverse as a legislature,
Sleep is as forward as hives or goiters,
And where it is least desired, it loiters.
Sleep is as shy as a maiden sprite,
And where it is most desired, takes flight.
So people who go to bed to sleep
Must count French premiers or sheep,
And people who ought to arise from bed
Yawn and go back to sleep instead.

And you can pile all the poems in the world in a heap,
And this is the first to tell the truth about sleep.

What Almost Every Woman Knows
Sooner or Later

HUSBANDS are things that wives have to get used to putting up with,
And with whom they breakfast with and sup with.
They interfere with the discipline of nurseries,
And forget anniversaries,
And when they have been particularly remiss
They think they can cure everything with a great big kiss.
They are annoying when they stay home
And even more annoying when they roam,
And when you tell them about something they have done they just look unbearably patient and smile a superior smile,
And think, Oh she'll get over it after a while,
And they always drink cocktails faster than they can assimilate them,
And if you look in their direction they act as if they were martyrs and you were trying to sacrifice, or immolate them.
And when it's a question of walking five miles to play golf they are very energetic but if it's doing anything useful around the house they are very lethargic,
And then they tell you that women are unreasonable and don't know anything about logic,

And they never want to get up or go to bed at the same time as you do,

And when you perform some simple common or garden rite like putting cold cream on your face or applying a touch of lipstick they seem to think you are up to some kind of black magic like a priestess of Voodoo,

And if you serve meat balls for dinner they look put-upon and say Can't we ever have a sirloin or a porterhouse,

So you get them what they want and then when the bills come in they act as if you were trying to drive them to the slorterhouse,

And they are brave and calm and cool and collected about the ailments of the person they have promised to honor and cherish,

But the minute they get a sniffle or a stomach-ache of their own, why you'd think they were about to perish,

And when you are alone with them they ignore all the minor courtesies and as for airs and graces, they utterly lack them,

But when there are a lot of people around they hand you so many chairs and ash trays and sandwiches and butter you with such bowings and scrapings that you want to smack them.

Husbands are indeed an irritating form of life,

And yet through some quirk of Providence most of them are really very deeply ensconced in the affection of their wife.

Turns in a Worm's Lane

I'VE never bet on a so-called horse
    That the horse didn't lose a leg.
I've never putted on a golfing course
But the ball behaved like an egg.
I've never possessed three royal kings
But somebody held three aces;
In short, I'm a lad whose presence brings
The joy to bankers' faces.

And everybody says, "What a splendid loser!"
Everybody says, "What a thoroughgoing sport!"
And I smile my smile like an amiable Duse,
I leer like a lawyer in the presence of a tort.
And I crack my lips,
And I grin my grin,
While someone else
Rakes my money in.
Yes, I smile a smile like the Mona Lisa,
Though my spirits droop like the Tower of Pisa.
Yes, I chortle like a military march by Sousa
And everybody says, "What a splendid loser!"

I'll buy a tome, an expensive tome,
On the gentle craft of diddling,
And I'll wrap it up and I'll take it home,
And read till I'm fair to middling.

I'll stealthily study the ebony arts
Of men like the great Houdini,
Till both in foreign and local parts
I'm known as a darned old meany.

And everyone will say, "What a nasty winner!"
And everyone will say, "What a dreadful sport!"
And they'll all stop inviting me to come to dinner,
For I used to be a dimple and I want to be a wart.

But I won't care,
And I'll win with a scowl,
Foul means or fair,
But preferably foul.

I'll jeer my victims every time I vanquish,
And if I lose I shall scream with anguish.
And people will say, "What a dreadful sport!"
And I'll say, "Phooie!" or something of the sort.

Requiem

THERE was a young belle of old Natchez
    Whose garments were always in patchez.
When comment arose
On the state of her clothes,
She drawled, When Ah itchez, Ah scratchez!

Bernarr Macfadden

Bernarr Macfadden has given the preamble to the
Constitution a sequel,
And established the fact that all women are created
physiqual.
What is more, he has logically developed a little-known
theory of Rousseau's;
Viz: that there is a definite connection between fine
torsos and fine trousseaux.
Yes, many a tenor or baritone has succumbed to some
contralto or soprano
Who learned from Mr. Macfadden about *mens sana in
corpore sano.*
As a publisher he invariably puts his trust
In a picture of a thigh or a bust.
Perhaps the idea was impromptu
But look what he has comptu!
He could now, if he wished, celebrate every Epiphany
By purchasing a fine solitaire diamond from Mr. Tiffany;
Or again, if he so desired, he could buy for each of his
friends on Septuagesima
A steel girder or turret from the works of Bessemer.
That's what the human body if properly exploited is
capable of.
What is this thing called love?

May I Drive You Home,
Mrs. Murgatroyd?

Here's a statement that anybody who feels so inclined is welcome to make a hearty mental meal of:

People who possess operator's licenses ought never to ride in a car that anybody else is at the wheel of.

It seems to be their point of view

That you are some kind of fanatic bent on murdering or mutilating them even in the face of the certainty that in so doing you must murder or mutilate yourself too.

They are always jumping and wincing and jamming their feet down on an imaginary brake,

Or making noises as if they had just discovered that their bed was inhabited by a snake,

Or else they start a casual conversation that begins with remarks about the weather and other banalities,

And leads up to a pointed comment on the horrifying number of annual automobile fatalities.

They tell you not only about cars that actually are coming but also cars that might be coming, and they do it so kindly and gently

That it's obvious they consider you deaf and blind as well as rather deficient mently.

And when at last you somehow manage to get to where you've been going to they say thank you in a voice full of plaster of Paris and bitter aloes,

And get down out of the car as if they were getting down
    off the gallows,
And they walk away with the Is-it-really-over expression
    of a lot of rescued survivors
And you go off and make a lot of remarks to yourself
    about back-seat drivers,
And you vow that come what may you yourself will
    never join their ranks, no indeed,
And then the next day somebody gives you a lift and you
    find yourself bathed with cold moisture the moment
    they shift the gears into third speed.
The truth of the matter, mesdames and sirs,
Is that we are all born chauffeurs;
Or, to put it another way before retiring to curl up with
    a bad book on the sofa,
Everybody in the car can drive better than the chauffeur.

So Penseroso

COME, megrims, mollygrubs and collywobbles!
     Come, gloom that limps, and misery that hobbles!
Come also, most exquisite melancholiage,
As dark and decadent as November foliage!
I crave to shudder in your moist embrace,
To feel your oystery fingers on my face.
This is my hour of sadness and of soulfulness,
And cursed be he who dissipates my dolefulness.
The world is wide, isn't it?
The world is roomy.
Isn't there room, isn't it,
For a man to be gloomy?
Bring me a bathysphere, kindly,
Maybe like Beebe's,
Leave me alone in it, kindly,
With my old heebie-jeebies.
I do not desire to be cheered,
I desire to retire, I am thinking of growing a beard,
A sorrowful beard, with a mournful, a dolorous hue in it,
With ashes and glue in it.
I want to be drunk with despair,
I want to caress my care,
I do not wish to be blithe,
I wish to recoil and writhe,
I will revel in cosmic woe,
And I want my woe to show.
This is the morbid moment,

This is the ebony hour.
Aroint thee, sweetness and light!
I want to be dark and sour!
Away with the bird that twitters!
All that glitters is jitters!
Roses, roses are gray,
Violets cry Boo! and frighten me.
Sugar is diabetic,
And people conspire to brighten me.
Go hence, people, go hence!
Go sit on a picket fence!
Go gargle with mineral oil,
Go out and develop a boil!
Melancholy is what I brag and boast of,
Melancholy I mean to make the most of,
You beaming optimists shall not destroy it.
But while I am it, I intend to enjoy it.
Go, people, feed on kewpies and soap,
And remember, please, that when I mope, I mope!

The Purist

I GIVE you now Professor Twist,
   A conscientious scientist.
Trustees exclaimed, "He never bungles!"
And sent him off to distant jungles.
Camped on a tropic riverside,
One day he missed his loving bride.
She had, the guide informed him later,
Been eaten by an alligator.
Professor Twist could not but smile.
"You mean," he said, "a crocodile."

Everybody Eats Too Much Anyhow

You gulp your breakfast and glance at the clock,
　　Through eleventh hour packing you gallop amok,
You bundle your bags in the back of the car,
You enter, she enters, and there you are.
You clutch the wheel, she clutches the maps,
And longs for a couple of extra laps.
It's au revoir to your modest abode,
You're gipsies, away on the open road;
Into the highway you burst like a comet or
Heat waves climbing a Kansas thermometer.
The conversation is sweet as clover,
With breakfast practically hardly over.
'Darling, light me a cigarette?"
"At once and with all my heart, my pet;
"And by the way, we are off the track;
"We should have turned left a half-mile back."
You swing around with a cheery smile,
Thus far, a mile is only a mile.
The road is romance, so let it wind,
With breakfast an hour or so behind.
Under the tires the pebbles crunch,
And through the dust creep thoughts of lunch.
The speedometer sits on a steady fifty
And more and more does lunch seem nifty.
Your eyes to the road ahead are glued,
She glances about in search of food.
She sees a place. She would like to try it.

She says so. Well, you're already by it.
Ignoring the road, you spot an eatery;
The look of it makes her interior teetery.
She sees a beauty. You're past it again.
Her eyebrows look like ten past ten;
She's simmering now, and so are you,
And your brows register ten to two.
She snubs the excuse as you begin it:
That there'll be another one any minute,
She says there won't. It must be a plot;
She's absolutely correct. There's not.
You finally find one. You stop and alight.
You're both too annoyed to eat a bite.
Oh, this is the gist of my gipsy song:
Next time carry your lunch along.

Just a Piece of Lettuce and Some Lemon Juice, Thank You

THE human body is composed
   Of head and limbs and torso,
Kept slim by gents
At great expense,
By ladies, even more so.

The human waistline will succumb
To such and such a diet.
The ladies gnaw
On carrots raw,
Their husbands will not try it.

The human bulk can be compressed
By intricate devices,
Which ladies hie
In droves to buy
At pre-depression prices.

The human shape can be subdued
By rolling on the floor.
Though many wives
Thus spend their lives,
To husbands it's a bore.

Though human flesh can be controlled,
We're told, by this and that,
You cannot win:
The thin stay thin,
The fat continue fat.

Allergy Met a Bear

I HEARD them speak of allergy,
  I asked them to explain,
Which when they did, I asked them
To please explain again.

I found the pith of allergy
In Bromides tried and true;
For instance, you like lobster,
But lobster don't like you.

Does aspirin cause your eyes to cross?
Do rose-leaves make you nervy?
Do old canaries give you boils?
Do kittens give you scurvy?

Whatever turns your skin to scum,
Or turns your blood to glue,
Why, that's the what, the special what,
That you're allergic to.

O allergy, sweet allergy,
Thou lovely word to me!
Swift as an heiress Reno-bound
I called on my M.D.

This doctor was obliged to me
For reasons I must edit.

(I knew he had two extra wives,
And neither did him credit.)

I spoke to him of allergy;
Perhaps I clenched my fist;
But when I left his domicile
I had a little list.

I can't attend the opera now,
Or sleep within a tent;
I cannot ride in rumble seats;
My allergies prevent.

Oh, garden parties speed my pulse
And pound my frame to bits;
I'd mind the child on Thursdays,
But children give me fits.

When Duty sounds her battle cry,
Say never that I shirk;
It isn't laziness at all,
But an allergy to work.

An Introduction to Dogs

THE dog is man's best friend.
　　He has a tail on one end.
Up in front he has teeth.
And four legs underneath.

Dogs like to bark.
They like it best after dark.
They not only frighten prowlers away
But also hold the sandman at bay.

A dog that is indoors
To be let out implores.
You let him out and what then?
He wants back in again.

Dogs display reluctance and wrath
If you try to give them a bath.
They bury bones in hideaways
And half the time they trot sideaways.

They cheer up people who are frowning,
And rescue people who are drowning,
They also track mud on beds,
And chew people's clothes to shreds.

Dogs in the country have fun.
They run and run and run.

But in the city this species
Is dragged around on leashes.

Dogs are upright as a steeple
And much more loyal than people.
Well people may be reprehensibler
But that's probably because they are sensible

To a Small Boy Standing on My Shoes
While I Am Wearing Them

LET's straighten this out, my little man,
    And reach an agreement if we can.
I entered your door as an honored guest.
My shoes are shined and my trousers are pressed,
And I won't stretch out and read you the funnies
And I won't pretend that we're Easter bunnies.
If you must get somebody down on the floor,
What in the hell are your parents for?
I do not like the things that you say
And I hate the games that you want to play.
No matter how frightfully hard you try,
We've little in common, you and I.
The interest I take in my neighbor's nursery
Would have to grow, to be even cursory,
And I would that performing sons and nephews
Were carted away with the daily refuse,
And I hold that frolicsome daughters and nieces
Are ample excuse for breaking leases.
You may take a sock at your daddy's tummy
Or climb all over your doting mummy,
But keep your attentions to me in check
Or, sonny boy, I will wring your neck.
A happier man today I'd be
Had someone wrung it ahead of me.

A Drink with Something in It

THERE is something about a Martini,
  A tingle remarkably pleasant;
A yellow, a mellow Martini;
I wish that I had one at present.
There is something about a Martini,
Ere the dining and dancing begin,
And to tell you the truth,
It is not the vermouth—
I think that perhaps it's the Gin.

There is something about an old-fashioned
That kindles a cardiac glow;
It is soothing and soft and impassioned
As a lyric by Swinburne or Poe.
There is something about an old-fashioned
When dusk has enveloped the sky,
And it may be the ice,
Or the pineapple slice,
But I strongly suspect it's the Rye.

There is something about a mint julep.
It is nectar imbibed in a dream,
As fresh as the bud of the tulip,
As cool as the bed of the stream.
There is something about a mint julep,
A fragrance beloved by the lucky.

And perhaps it's the tint
Of the frost and the mint,
But I think it was born in Kentucky.

There is something they put in a highball
That awakens the torpidest brain,
That kindles a spark in the eyeball,
Gliding singing through vein after vein.
There is something they put in a highball
Which you'll notice one day, if you watch;
And it may be the soda,
But judged by the odor,
I rather believe it's the Scotch.

Then here's to the heartening wassail,
Wherever good fellows are found;
Be its master instead of its vassal,
And order the glasses around.
Oh, it's Beer if you're bent on expansion,
And Wine if you wish to grow thin,
But quaffers who think
Of a drink as a drink,
When they quaff, quaff of Whisky and Gin.

Index of First Lines

–[246]–